A Celebration of Willow

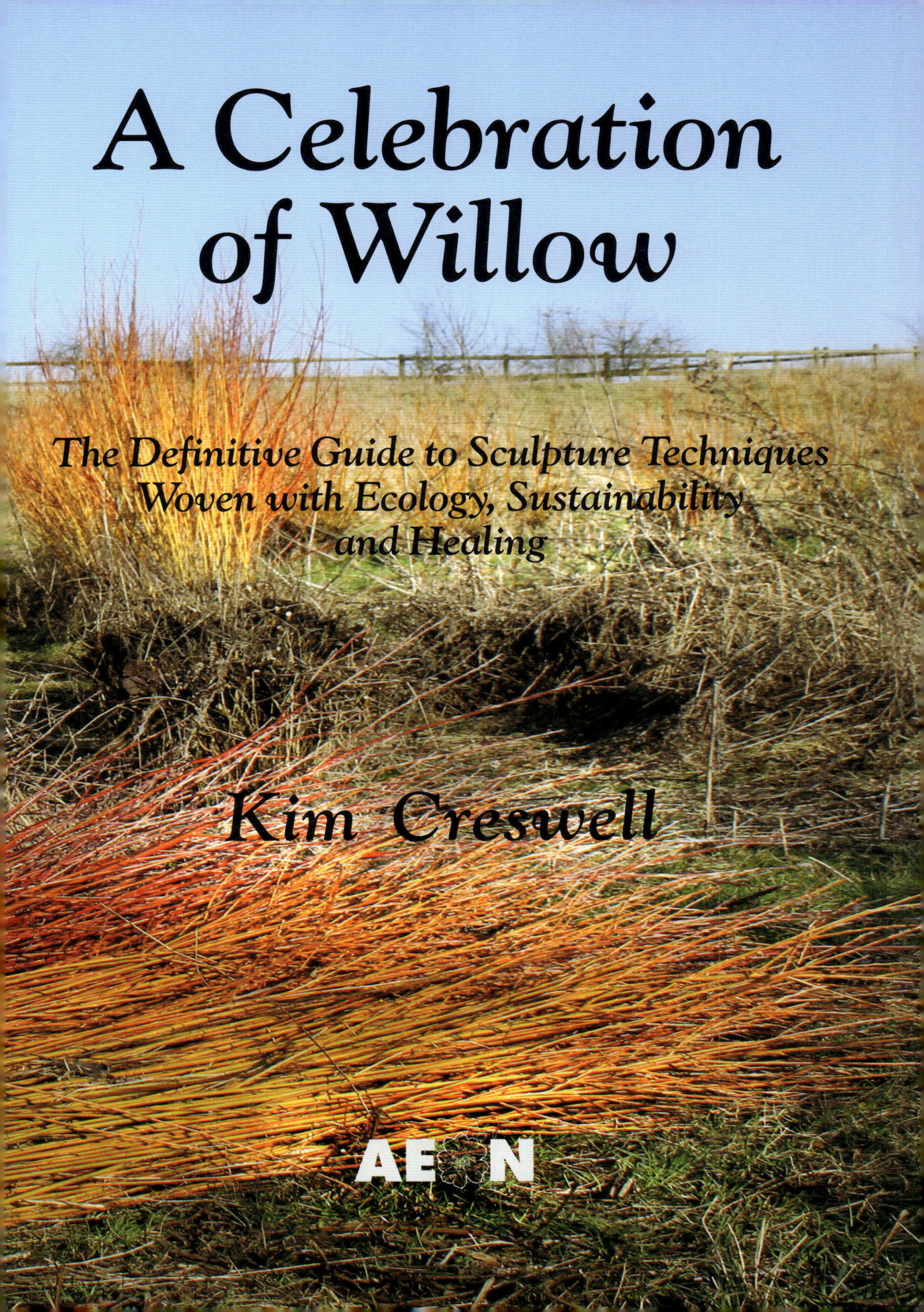

A Celebration of Willow

The Definitive Guide to Sculpture Techniques Woven with Ecology, Sustainability and Healing

Kim Creswell

AEON

First published in 2024 by
Aeon Books Ltd

Copyright © 2024 by Kim Creswell

The right of Kim Creswell to be identified as the author of this work has been asserted in accordance with §§ 77 and 78 of the Copyright Design and Patents Act 1988.

All rights reserved. No part of this publication may be reproduced, stored in a retrieval system, or transmitted, in any form or by any means, electronic, mechanical, photocopying, recording, or otherwise, without the prior written permission of the publisher.

British Library Cataloguing in Publication Data

A C.I.P. for this book is available from the British Library

ISBN: 978–1–80152–051–5

Printed in Great Britain by Bell and Bain Ltd, Glasgow

www.aeonbooks.co.uk

*Dedicated to Rowan and Oakley,
my pride and my joy.*

*In solidarity with all brave environmentalists,
who know true riches cannot be measured in money.*

Contents

	Introduction	1
1	Ecology	11
2	Willow, the healer	17
3	Sourcing your materials	29
	Growing willow	29
	Pathogens	33
	Managing the withy bed	34
	Harvesting the withy bed	39
	Sorting and storing	43
	Hedges	45
	Gardens	48
	Willow merchants	48
	Preparation	50
4	Basic techniques	53
	The anatomy of willow	53
	Willow ties and wraps	54
	Willow sculpture techniques	59
	Basketry techniques	66
	Woodwork	68
	Preserving	72
5	Weaving a willow goose	75
	Willow goose foundations	77
	Adding the legs	94
	Willow goose finishing	100

6	**Weaving a willow pig**	**107**
	Willow pig foundations	*108*
	Adding the legs	*115*
	Willow pig finishing	*127*
7	**Weaving a willow stag on a hedgerow frame**	**139**
	Making the frame	*143*
	Creating the shape	*147*
	Adding the detail	*153*
8	**Metal frames**	**159**
	Planning the metal frame	*160*
	Making the metal frame	*163*
	Preserving the sculpture	*172*
9	**Weaving a living willow sculpture**	**181**
	Locating a living willow sculpture	*184*
	Planning the living willow sculpture	*201*
	Building the living willow sculpture	*206*
	Maintaining a living willow sculpture	*215*
10	**Weaving willow figures**	**219**
	Conclusion	**231**

GLOSSARY	233
A HERBAL BIBLIOGRAPHY	237
INDEX	239

A Celebration of Willow

Photo by Steven Wooster

Introduction

Growing up by the banks of both the River Wey and the Wey Navigation Canal, I must have played in the shade of willows throughout my childhood, without realising what an important part of my life the plant would become.

A wild sort of child I was, favouring running through woods, building dens, and making potions out of plants over sitting indoors playing with dollies. I felt more at home in the great outdoors than in a brick box. Sadly, during my formative teenage years I was witness to the destruction wrought upon the ancient Wisley Woods and surrounding ecosystems by the crazy obsession with road building, and I decided that I did not want to support a system that prioritised personal greed over the natural world.

The path calling to me lay in making, but being part of "the system" meant forgoing my heart's cries. This led to the purchase of a dodgy old Transit van in 1990, determined to travel the country, painting what I saw.

Being skint, and by no means mechanically minded, led inevitably to the breakdown of said van and the unsought-for permanent halt in an Oxford car park. When one morning I woke up lying in a puddle of rainwater from the leaking van roof, some neighbouring travelling people offered to show me how to build a "bender tent" – a traditional Gypsy dwelling made from arched, coppiced hazel rods, with a canvas tarpaulin slung over the top. As it happened, there were no coppiced hazel rods growing in the vicinity, but there was a fallen willow tree on an abandoned Victorian rubbish dump. From its stump

Photo by Steven Wooster

had grown rods, straight, strong, and very bendy. Those rods we cut to make a tent frame, then covered this with some found old plastic sheets. The construction provided adequate shelter from the elements.

Now that was a cold winter, with temperatures regularly down to −8 °C. One particularly memorable night, a storm took the cover and left me in bed looking up at wild, starry skies while my few possessions blew away around me. Though I had no wood burner for warmth, I did have three large dogs (and the occasional company of a grumpy billy goat) who kept me from hypothermia.

When spring shone, it was definitely time to change my view and change my luck. As I dismantled the simple structure that had been my home for the winter, I noticed that the willow rods had taken root, with tiny leaf buds emerging along their length. This observation immediately led to what I can only describe as a "light-bulb moment". I suddenly envisaged sculptures made of willow trees; these were shapes that lived, breathed, and grew, way beyond the input of the sculptor, sculptures that took on their own lives, absorbing and reflecting the environmental variabilities that every living thing is subject to. I pictured people walking through forests of trees that grew like horses, wondering if those trees had freakishly purposed themselves.

Certainly my life did change dramatically from that moment. I found myself with a Rowan seed in my belly, and the following winter I gave birth to my daughter in a caravan, down an old ox drove, under the branches of an oak tree.

When Rowan turned one, we exchanged the bus in which we were living for a wagon-horse and a spinner cart. I returned to bender life with my baby in the company of a horse, who took the weight of our chattels, firewood, and spring water.

I had the good fortune to share this nomadic lifestyle with many finely skilled rural artisans. We sold our wares on the side of the road as we travelled.

It was during this time that I began to revisit and manifest my ideas of willow sculpture, experimenting with shape and form, using the sticks, herbage, and withies which were abundant as we moved through the countryside.

As time went on, a display of willow sculptures and hedgerow baskets was ever-present outside the wagon, as we stopped on verges and commons. Those displays made us approachable, and there was

Picture by Steven Wooster

often a stream of interested people stopping for a chat and to browse the unique hand-made items, created from the very land we were standing on. The friendly support of these good folk facilitated the continued development of my ideas and techniques.

I began by making small items, such as pigs and geese, developing techniques for detailed anatomical shapes, and working sympathetically with hand-collected natural materials. In this book I share with you the techniques that I have developed and refined over the last thirty years. If you can make a pig and a goose, then you can pretty much make anything!

My sculptures became well known as we travelled the lanes with our horse, wagon, and woven wares. Locals would ask if I'd prune their gardens in return for the willow, and suddenly I found myself with stacks of coppiced willow and no way to move it. There was far too much to put on the cart – my poor old horse would've been on his knees!

The glut of materials prompted me to "weave big", and I began to construct a "life-sized" (because they are real, y'know) unicorn on the wayside greensward, while the kettle was bubbling on the stick fire. To me, unicorns symbolise joyful freedom, creativity, and the successful pursuit of dreams. Three different people invited that sculpture into their garden, prompting the creation of further unicorns, and then a couple of years of making many unicorns with different specifics. This repetition facilitated development of frame techniques, muscular representation, and a wider exploration of living willow sculpture.

I held my first willow workshop in 1999, at the request of some passers-by. We spent a sunny spring day sitting by a stream, amongst the primroses, and it was there that I saw the deep therapeutic values of working with willow. All plants have their own characteristics, you may even say personalities. Willow is a plant that seems to be deeply nurturing and able to offer strong, yet flexible, support. Since that first sylvan sculpture session, I have instructed over a thousand people in willow sculpture, and I love to watch the subtle movements of emotion as the willow is woven. I find this more prominent when using fresh willow, but it is still present to some extent when the willow has been stored and soaked.

After being mainly home-educated, my daughter requested school attendance in 2003 – a decision that required us to become sedentary. I was keen to keep our low-impact lifestyle, so I bought a plot of land

at auction and began to develop an off-grid, organically run smallholding and nature reserve. As a template for management I used the old-fashioned biodiverse common, which we, during our wagon days, so often used to call home. A withy bed was planted, with gathered cuttings, to supply materials for commissions and classes. The encompassing hedges were traditionally laid, following roughly fifty years of flailing, and reinstated as an invaluable resource for man and beast.

The burgeoning hedgerow and flourishing of species, on the previously mono-crop plot, offered provisions for the continuance of food foraging and medicine making. Serendipity took me by the hand in 2015 and led me down the path of rigorous medical herbalism training, which has allowed me to add a whole new layer to my intimate relationship with willow.

Since the 1990s a new industry has developed, that of willow sculpture. No doubt folk would have made figures from willow, to represent their life experience, but I suggest that in times gone by practical willow items, such as baskets, were more necessary to ordinary life. As a society, we have suffered a strange shift that has removed us from our daily dose of nature . . . our place of belonging. We no longer handle the well-worn withies of a shopper every time we step out of the door. All has become plastic, and with that we feel a yearning, sometimes unheard but always there. I suggest that this is what has led to the rise in popularity of willow sculpting, a seeking for reconnection with our true natures. Willow offers to be our guide.

In this book I would like to share my own willow sculpture techniques with you, along with many other gifts that my dear plant ally has shared to reconnect people with planet. The generosity of *Salix* knows no bounds but is not to be taken for granted. No plant or animal is "under our dominion". Every living being has its own thing going on; their priority is not our benefit.

I have compiled and included a Glossary at the end of the book, to which you can refer as you read and make, if terms are unfamiliar.

* * *

This book is a celebration of Willow and how she allows us to connect with ourselves as part of nature. We people are relative newcomers to this planet; we have evolved as part of this complex web of life, and this I urge you to consciously acknowledge every time you hold a willow wand. Nurturing is Mother Nature, and fortunate we are indeed.

Photo by Chris Groves

1

Ecology

Stumble into an unkempt patch of wet woodland, and it can be as if stepping back into prehistory, a taste of untamed wilderness: squelchy underfoot, with animal tracks creating faint paths through tussocks of sedge and leaf-filled pools; stumps of rotting wood providing plinths for mosses, ferns, and trailing ivy. In the kingdom of the carr, you'll find willow a predominant pioneer.

Although an ancient landscape, having developed widely as glaciers retreated, these carrs are generally not a permanent geographical feature, but more a dynamic phase of an ever-changing terrain. Pioneer species, such as willow, birch, and alder, dry the ground and increase humus, allowing development of a forest of other species, such as oak and ash, while the shifting geology moves the wetland resource elsewhere.

It's easy for us quick-living humans to assume that things were always as we find them, but Earth has her own rhythms and cycles, generally slower and therefore unrecognised by us, unless scrutinised. Steady evolutionary processes can be influenced by faster-moving natural events or traditional management practices, which nature has resilience strategies for and can often flourish from – quite different from the mindless devastation caused by some of mankind's less enlightened activities.

Traditional land management practices, such as coppicing, allowed exploitation of resources while supporting existing wildlife populations, with many woodlands being shaped over centuries by humans working synergistically with the natural environs and all its inhabitants.

Vast acreages of wet woodland have been lost in recent decades, largely due to drainage for agriculture and development. Inevitably, this has led to the sudden and dramatic decline of many species. We human beings can no longer plead ignorance. We are well aware of what we do and how to do things better – poor show from the powers that be, who do not adequately address obvious problems with policy. With this chronic and appalling failure of leadership, I suggest that it falls to we people on the ground to step up and act, to create positive change. If everyone did a little, then that little would be a lot!

Three-year-old willow, planted to prevent bank erosion, also providing wildlife habitat, basketry osiers, and bright winter colour.

Willow is seen as a keystone taxon – the *Salix* genus comprises many diverse species, distributed over a wide area, presenting benefit to a huge array of insects, birds, amphibians, and mammals. Willow's humble and ubiquitous nature belies her true character. Ruled by the moon and associated with nurture, native willows in Britain are known to support a huge and varied number of insects, which, in turn, form the basis of a large and diverse food chain. No wonder, then, that many animals have evolved alongside willow and are reliant on her presence for their very existence.

In a healthy landscape, which also provides for the over-populated human species, it is important to allow diversity within all areas. There is nothing sensible about a monoculture. A case may be made for extensive reintroduction of carr areas, which would provide benefits in biodiversity, mitigating flood risk, reducing atmospheric pollutants, and helping to filter run-off contamination from agriculture and development.

Where ground is needed for production, then short rotation coppice (SRC) may be a viable solution to some supply-and-demand challenges. Of course it is important not to put willow plantations where they shouldn't be, as replacing other declining habitats with them would be ludicrous, but a well-managed willow SRC can provide a biodiverse and abundant nature reserve while at the same time providing resources for people: it does not have to be "either–or".

As well as supplying many important artisan industries, SRC willow is a viable, yet massively underutilised, biofuel. Widespread investment in willow growing would, directly and indirectly, reduce reliance on fossil fuels, as well as providing skilled work for local people and essential goods for the local economy, based on environmentally sustainable production methods.

It is bonkers that we in the UK have removed the vast majority of our historic withy beds and have, for several decades, had to import enough osiers for our needs. There has never been a more important time to support local, ethically sound businesses that prioritise regeneration of natural habitat.

2

Willow, the healer

Willow was already old when our species was in its infancy. We have developed with her, side by side, through generations, from cradle to grave.

Given that herbal medicine has been used by people for as long as there have been people, and that willow is widespread, I feel on firm ground speculating that the healing properties of willow have been utilised for all of our time. Historical accounts of willow are found from earliest civilisations. Certainly *Salix* was used in ancient Greece and Rome and was written about by early scholars.

Astrology and medicine have been intertwined since ancient days, up until a few hundred years ago, as we began to fully divorce ourselves from nature. The interactions of celestial bodies, meandering through the solar system, are seen to influence life on Earth. Each of those circulating entities has been observed, over millennia, to govern conditions on macro and micro levels, patterns being consistent and recognisable wherever they are.

Western medicine tradition was founded on the ancient Greek humoral* system, which named four constitutional types. Each person is ascribed a dominant constitutional type, seen with a predisposition to certain conditions. During the 1800s, humoral medicine fell out of favour, with emphasis then put on the microorganisms that cause disease. However, humoral-style medicine can go some way to explaining why different people faced with the same pathogens react in different ways.

The heating, drying, cooling, or moistening properties of foods, medicines, seasonal patterns, and cosmic influences were seen to exert

> **A note on humoral medicine:* Ancient civilisations developed similar approaches and sentiments to the causes and relief of disease independently across the world.
>
> *I postulate that the humoral medicine system may not be dissimilar to the approaches of ancient Brits. Unlike some other cultures, we have not retained an unbroken tradition of herbal medicine, but the old knowledge is still there, bubbling under the surface.*
>
> *The four constitutional types and their associated humours (bodily fluids) are: phlegmatic (phlegm), sanguine (blood), choleric (yellow bile), and melancholic (black bile). The four associated elements are, respectively: water, air, fire, and earth, which are united by ether.*
>
> *As willow is associated with water, she falls firmly into the phlegmatic constitution: cold and moist, representing parts of the body including lymph fluid, the eyes, and the lungs, bladder, and kidneys, supporting nourishment, movement, and elimination.*

distinct pressures on people. Collated information could provide forewarning, diagnosis, prognosis, and treatment strategies, with a physician aiming to restore good health through balance of the patient's constitution.

To this end, medicinal plants were "given" to, or "owned" by planets, which were associated with certain traits. In days when most education was carried out verbally, attributing personalities to plants and planets must have been an invaluable method of ensuring continuance of vital knowledge and experience gained through generations.

The personalities given to plants in prehistoric times still ring true and deep within our society's psyche: still there but secret, hidden in plain sight, waiting to be rediscovered. With each plant that calls you, or strangely enters your life, I urge you to sit a while, take some time, get to know each other. Allow yourself the time to go at your plant ally's pace. Just as with people, you may not get on with every plant, but some you will joyfully resonate with. You will have your own unique relationship with the plants you meet, while sharing their broader characteristics with many other admirers.

Willow is happiest by the water, where she likes to stand. Her cooling character, appearance, and healing abilities bind her closely with the moon, who represents the feminine.

The moon exerts her pull on the Earth, the lunar cycle chiming with many women's menstrual cycle. Linked to fertility and motherhood, to the intuitive and emotional, the moon has a dreaming quality, as well as a shadow side, associated with the night and with animals such as the ethereal barn owl and the elusive hare.

Ice or steam, still and deep or burbling brook, expansive and awesome or tiny but powerful drops, water takes on many forms.

"Owl on Oak" (c. 2015).

"Winter Owl Hunting" (c. 2007).

Water element is characterised as cold and moist and likes to be fluid and moving. Stagnation is not good for water.

Willow's coppiced crown produces lithe and supple rods, whose strength lies in their flexibility. The moon's silvery colour is mirrored in the undersides of osier leaves as stools of maiden whips sway in the summer's breeze, their silver locks blowing with a whisper.

Willow can grow twisted, gnarly, and crone-like, her imposing figure standing by a flowing river: grandmother willow, shedding twigs and branches, carried by water and caught by the bank, saplings springing up downstream.

It has oft been said that willow is a tree of grief, with many poetical references associating willow with loss. This may be a simplification. Willow is a mover of emotions, consistent with the character of the moon and of water. Willow can stand by and flexibly support the flow of a grief process, or any other intense emotion, at whatever speed and force is appropriate.

Weaving with willow is especially therapeutic. There is something calming about the repetitive action, working with our prehistorically linked plant ally whose special gift is the unobtrusive aiding of emotional resolution. The steady to and fro, gently builds considered boundaries, creating a narrative that can comfortably be carried.

Willow has its own molecular fingerprint, which includes many constituents known to have medicinal benefits. Herbal medicine uses whole-plant parts, recognising that the highly evolved symphony of constituents creates a synergistic action, supporting complex physiological mechanisms that support homeostasis for health.

The most famous of willow's constituents is the phenolic compound salicylic acid, on which the synthesised "aspirin" is based. Natural salicylates and aspirin are both able to numb pain, reduce inflammation, and cool fevers, all features that are attributed to herbs

of the moon. Aspirin, however, has significant blood-thinning effects, as well as the potential to cause serious gastric damage, and even death, due to the alteration of the naturally occurring salicylic structure. By comparison, willow bark as a medicine has been found to be extremely safe. A small percentage of adults may experience a sensitivity to salicylates, manifesting in a gastric disturbance or rash, which stops upon cessation of the medicine. These reactions may be more severe in children, so it is recommended that children under 12 are not given *Salix*. Certain people are more likely to have a negative reaction to willow medicine, and for this reason such remedies should not be prescribed for asthmatics and folk with atopic tendencies. There is a theoretical risk that willow may potentiate the action of pharmaceutical

"Moongazing Hare" (c. 2012).

blood thinners, so it should not be used simultaneously with those. As with all medicinal preparations, it is important to know appropriate indications, contra-indications, and dosage advice. Cats cannot tolerate salicylates, so do not give them any willow.

The bark and leaves of the willow tree are high in tannins, which bind to protein molecules, tightening connective tissues. The dry, tight skin on a willow weaver's hands is testament to this, particularly when using pre-soaked willow, as the tannins of the bark are effectively extracted by water. Some tannins can be helpful in medicine: they aid with binding tissues, staunching blood flow, and drying secretions. One should be aware that tannins may prevent the absorption of nutrients, or co-administered medicine, through the intestinal walls.

The willow preparations that are most commonly found on the shelves of herbal medicine dispensaries in modern Britain are tinctures of the bark of *Salix alba* (white willow), or *S. purpurea* (purple willow). The bark of the young branches of those two species has particularly vibrant colouring, pigments that are indicative of groups of medically active flavonoids.

Any of the willows may be used medicinally, as they all contain roughly the same range of constituents. Seasonal variations will influence what is available to harvest. Bark, young twigs, leaves, aments (the furry flowers), seeds, and sap may all be used. Herbs should be gathered when completely dry if storage is intended.

Flowers may be collected from mid-winter into spring, as the plant begins to wake from its winter slumber. Flowers are best used fresh, decocted in water or wine; they are a traditional remedy for curbing conditions associated with sexual excess, such as rapid or unwanted ejaculation, as well as conditions associated with inflammation in the genitourinary tract – conditions that may be seen as an excess of heat, in areas associated and consistent with the expulsive, flowing qualities of the moon and water. The flowers of the willow, as the tree's reproductive organs, are able to share their hormone-balancing properties with us, and the nature of the tree cools down heated conditions.

As willow flowers appear, sap is beginning to rise. The plant's life-blood can be collected by drilling a small hole and inserting a tube to syphon the liquid from under the bark. It is vital, though, that the hole is properly plugged before too much is taken, or the tree may bleed to death. The liquid, packed with phytochemicals, has been a remedy for eye conditions – eyes being a part of the body associated with the phlegmatic constitution, seeing, and intuition. Cataracts,

The full moon shines brightly through the leaves of this eared willow (Salix aurita), so called because she has small, ear-like stipules along the shoots. This tree planted herself next to my cabin, and offers indispensable shade in the summer, protection from south-westerly winds, and is favoured by an array of small and joyful birds. We call her the listening willow, but she whispers too.

which cause darkening of vision, rheumy eyes that water, heated redness and irritation, all call for willow's cool moon medicine.

Leaves are available in quantity throughout the summer months and can be used fresh, or dried for storage. As with the bark and the seeds, being high in tannins, the leaves are excellent for staunching blood flow, both internally and externally. An infusion (in water or wine) may be used as a topical application, helping to heal wounds and running ulcers. The brew can be drunk to slow heavy menstrual bleeding, with salicylates offering pain relief for associated cramping. Traditionally this herb has been used for staying the coughing up of blood associated with tuberculosis. The leaves, along with flowers and seeds, can act as an anaphrodisiac in cases where inflamed passions present a problem. The herb cools and controls flow, with affinity to the menstrual cycle and the lungs, consistent with the attributes of the watery moon.

Bark, when harvested, should not be stripped straight from the tree, but taken from one- or two-year-old branches once they have been carefully removed from the plant. The chemical profile of any herb is variable, as it deals with survival requirements in real time. The salicin content of bark is generally highest at the end of the spring, which is also the time when the bark can most easily be stripped from the stick. If you are collecting in order to store and you are collecting it primarily for salicylate content, the time to gather is from the middle to the end of spring, although there will be active constituents throughout the year. I find it is helpful to be flexible when working with willow.

The bark can be decocted and used in the base of an anti-inflammatory and anodyne cream for muscle and joint aches, or a saucepan full of strained decoction can be poured into the bath after a day's digging. Young twigs contain constituents found in the bark and can be used the same way. Willow bark, like the seeds, may be dried, powdered, and used as a styptic wound powder.

Freshly stripped willow bark.

Willow bark and chopped young twigs, drying for storage and medicine-making.

Willow has developed sensible survival mechanisms. It is very bitter and extremely drying, so large quantities have undesirable effects on mucous membranes all the way through the digestive system, due to the binding effects of the tannins. There are other salicylate-containing plants that may be more appropriate for internal use. However, willow can be helpful for easing pain and inflammation associated with rheumatism, particularly in those cases exacerbated by damp conditions, and of excessive menstrual flow with cramping. Willow bark may be prepared as a vinegar or tincture and added to herbal medicine formulas, allowing concentrated, regular dosage without the adverse effects caused by ingesting quantity.

Moon mother willow provides abundant nurturing, physically, emotionally, and spiritually. She soothes our pain, cools our heat, clears our vision, and supports our frazzled emotions. Her generosity knows no bounds. This ancient being offers embracing strength, flexibility, and empathy: a dear friend and trusted teacher indeed!

* * *

This chapter was planned while sitting by the window of a rural wooden cabin, beside coppiced willow waiting to be cut, in the midst of the phlegmatic season, between Imbolc and the spring equinox.

The writing process began as the moon waxed full, the creative process supported by the expansive energy offered by Luna's gravitational pull. As the moon began to wane, I could retreat from the words to tidy and tweak. It was a powerful time of manifestation.

During this birthing process I was delighted and enchanted by the presence of a beautiful doe hare, epitome of the luna feminine. She arrived during the full moon and passed this special time alongside me. Today she has been loping around the cabin, nibbling grass and chasing pheasants. She stretched out her arms and legs, carefully grooming her elegant tan body and soft, pale underbelly. Now she sits, hunkered down in the short-grazed grass, aside some coppiced willow, butt-end into the south-westerly wind, black-tipped ears laid flat against her back. I have a feeling that when I'm done, she will be gone. I am so very grateful for a visit from Willow's moon goddess.

* * *

If you would like to dive more deeply into Willow's medicinal, magical, and mythical properties you may like to study the works named in the herbal bibliography, which is found at the end of this book.

3

Sourcing your materials

Growing willow

Historically speaking, just about every settlement would have had its own supply of osiers, and traces of this history can still be seen, especially near water courses on old common land, where willow trees were often pollarded above grazing height. The villagers could turn out their animals to graze the shared space and still have a harvest of uneaten withies to cut during the winter.

Osiers for weaving are coppiced annually, cut close to the ground for maximum growth. Willows may be pollarded, making the cut higher up the stem. Pollarding allows the new shoots to grow above the height of browsing herbivores and can be useful when marking and protecting the edges of watercourses. Multiple stems grow from the point of the cut, creating what is known as a "stool" or a "crown".

Choose species of willow that are appropriate for your plot – varieties that are suitable for your purposes and will thrive in the conditions you are offering. You may like to plant a single row, or stagger planting for denser lines. Planting in a block of straight lines, with paths between the rows, allows ease of maintenance and harvest while encouraging strong upward growth, but you can, of course, plant in any shape that works for you. One day I'd love to plant

◀ *This withy bed is planted in rows with wide paths, allowing room for manoeuvre when harvesting.*

a willow Miz-Maze. There is something quite magical about losing yourself in a cooling labyrinth of waving willow, the sibilant leaves whispering in the shady summer breeze.

The most cost-effective way to initiate a withy bed is by using cuttings, which you can source yourself from established trees or buy from a supplier. Cuttings should be taken and planted during the winter months, when the plant is asleep. Take a freshly cut, one-year-old withy and cut into lengths of at least 30 cm (12 inches). Push these sticks straight into the ground to a depth of 20–25 cm (8–10 inches), and root growth will emerge from the leaf nodes that are under the ground. Try to push them in the right way up, although it won't always matter. By using cuttings of this length, rather than much longer rods, you will increase the success rate of the new plants, as the underdeveloped roots will find it easier supplying a shorter stem with nutrients.

Fresh cuttings, 30–40 cm (12–18 inches) in length, should be pushed straight into the ground over two thirds of their length.

The new plant is vulnerable to drought and to being outcompeted by perennials during the first two or three years. Although willow is hardy, the newly planted cuttings will require watering if weather conditions are dry for any length of time while leaves are on the plant. You may like to consider some kind of mulch around the base of each cutting, to help retain soil moisture and to prevent overbearing "weed" growth. I urge the use of naturally degradable mulches, such as wood chippings or cardboard. Woven plastic weed-suppressant sheets will inevitably break down into smaller pieces of plastic and never be completely removed.

When the plant has become established, you will find that watering and weed suppressant become unnecessary, as the extensive root system and powerful growth ensure the success of the *Salix*. Fallen leaves provide ground cover and nutrients that favour your coppiced trees. SRC requires no herbicide, pesticide, or fertiliser use.

Personally I do not cut the newly planted willow back for the first two winters, allowing its root system to become gently established.

Established coppiced willow shown growing from front to back. Left foreground shows a couple of rows planted one year previously, behind them a row of four-year-old coppiced plants.

From the third winter onwards the plant will be coppiced annually, providing an increased harvest each year, allowing for climactic variables. Estimated life expectancy of a coppiced willow stool is said to be about 50 years. I haven't outlived any of the willow trees I've planted yet, but each year new cuttings are added with a view to expansion and regeneration of the withy bed.

Pathogens

Willow is a hardy plant. I have never found it necessary to apply any artificial biocides or fertilisers. I have certainly had years where there has been black sooty mould present, a bit of canker, some orange rust, or a particular bug that becomes a feature, but I have never found the need to make the situation worse by adding poison.

Nature has its own balance, and that balance includes fungal forms and insect life – to exclude those is to deny trust in Mother Nature. Worth remembering is that plants and animals become susceptible to disease when stressed. My advice is to accept these cycles. If pathogens appear to be increasing, look at why your plants have become susceptible. A short-term solution may be seen as chemical control (although there are none specifically for willow fungi), but in the long term I suggest that you would be adding to the problem. Your role as a grower is to support a healthy ecosystem, not to poison the bits you find inconvenient.

Canker is a fungal infection that begins on the leaves and then spreads to the twig, showing as a change of texture on the bark. This will affect willow's ability to bend. Some years are worse than others, but I have never had a huge number of withies affected. If you see some on young shoots, you may like to cut out those rods that are infected.

Canker sores damage the structure of the willow, making it unsightly and unfit for bending.

Rust is a fungal infection that can result in leaf loss, but it should not become a problem if your plants are happy.

Black sooty mould may develop on the honeydew created by aphids and can look unsightly, but it is harmless to the plant and can be washed off the withy. Aphids are a crucial part of the biodiversity that the willow tree supports: I would be reluctant to attempt exclusion.

Managing the withy bed

When managing my withy bed, I look upon it as a shared resource and always try to consider the other creatures that depend on it for sustenance. This means I take great care with gentle maintenance and considerate harvest, and by never using biocides* in the area. By virtue of this approach the withy bed is a companionable place at all times of the year, whether it be small birds singing, weasels popping up from time to time, or unimpressed toads complaining when you move their leafy cover.

The concentration of life is so apparent, even during deep winter. The wrens, tits, and robins chatter amongst crisp lines of the yet-to-be coppiced willow, standing stark against the brisk, blue sky – brightly coloured bark made vibrant by the low golden sun. On those post-Imbolc days, as the willow first flowers, all dare to breathe a sigh of relief with a glimpse of the coming spring. The withy bed comes alive with the excited buzzing of insect inhabitants taking a needed sip of

---

*Biocides, such as the widely used organophosphate-based glyphosate products, were originally developed as weapons of chemical warfare, and were found to be useful in "controlling weeds and pests". Just as with the tobacco industry, manufacturers have repeatedly claimed their safety, despite the original development being specifically as a nerve agent. Now globally pervasive to the point of being found in rainwater, emerging evidence is documenting serious toxic effects to wildlife and people alike.

nectar from the fluffy pussy willows, when so little else is available.

Larger mammals are also welcome at the withy bed. However, deer and rabbits can be a little too enthusiastic at times, with their appetite for the fresh, young willow shoots. If repeatedly nibbled when coppice shoots first appear, even the most established *Salix* stool can decide to die. The willow is most vulnerable as new growth appears, and active steps should be taken to dissuade the deer and rabbits from decimating the crop.

"Roe Deer" (c. 2017).

The willow shown is cut above the height of grazing rabbits.

On no account would I think of excluding or exterminating our four-legged brethren, who are living their lives on the land where they were born. I have various strategies for compromise: my willows are coppiced at a height of about 18 inches from the ground, so the shoots can't be reached by browsing bunnies. If I'm concerned about deer, I visit the plantation at least every other day and, while I'm there, I'll take a pee at random points of the withy bed. Marking my territory lets the heorot know not to get too comfortable. I may cut some intrusive blackthorn branches and lay them across the cut stumps to provide protection against nibbling. It's all about balance: there is plenty enough to share if no one gets too greedy.

Foxes keep the rabbit numbers down, a natural and important part of balance. The badgers, so generous with sharing their space, have been here much longer than we have. The young ones tumble around during the summer months, so full of fun. Hares are fond of the withy bed. Despite their association with open plains, they like to leave their leverets in places of undisturbed, tussocky cover.

Buzzards circle on thermals above, and woodpeckers hammer on standing dead trees. Pipistrelle bats dart to and fro during the warmer evenings, revelling in the abundance of insect life. Toads rest in the damp cool of the willow stools. At night, the various hoots and squeals declare the presence of tawny owls, little owls, and barn owls.

Nature abhors a mono-crop: all species are dependent on diversity. Different varieties of willow offer varied characteristics,

"Barn Owl Quartering" (c. 2016).

"Badgers in the Meadow" (c. 2007).

which encourage an array of insects. Planting different species of *Salix* promotes a diversity of wildlife, offers the maker more scope for creation, and guards against devastating harvest loss from disease.

Just as having multiple types of willow, it is highly beneficial to include other types of native trees on your plot, with varying levels of maturity among the grove you are creating. Include decaying timber, areas of scrubby growth, and patches of perennial weeds, as all support diversity of flora and fauna.

It is possible to have a commercial crop and a wildlife haven, but best results will not be gained in isolation. Your neighbours' treatment of their land will inevitably impact yours, just as yours will theirs. Every living thing on our planet relies on other living things; we are all connected in our web of life. You may create the best habitat possible, but if next-door starts dousing biocides on centuries-old frog migration routes, destroying the habitat of breeding birds, shooting, or hunting with hounds for "sport", then you won't keep your happy, healthy wildlife for long. It is not sensible for society to rely on a few conscientious individuals to protect nature, but it is the duty of global governments, I would argue, to ensure legislative policy that protects ecosystems from harm.

Once plants are established, there is little to do throughout the year, as they take care of themselves very well indeed. You may choose to keep the paths clear of growth during the summer months, but if you do, please be very aware that there will be creatures everywhere. Motorised tools may not be the best idea. Although strimmers are efficient at cutting through soft growth, they can cause horrific injury to small animals. They also leave tiny pieces of plastic everywhere. A scythe, or shears, maybe more sympathetic to wildlife, while allowing you quiet and close communion. When cutting tall growth, I suggest that you pass over once with a long cut and then again, closer to the ground, when you can see what would have been hidden.

Harvesting the withy bed

The willow is dry, the sap is down, and there have been a few hard frosts, which brighten the colour of the bark – a perfect day for harvesting.

Firstly think of the bees! The pussy willow's furry flowers usually begin to appear in February, on last year's growth. These flowers provide a source of nectar vital to many pollinators, so please set aside an area of willow that you won't harvest – let's share!

When the sap is down and the tree is dormant, surgery is less stressful to the plant. Traditionally in the UK willow cutting takes place between November and March, although that period may be advisably shorter, depending on the weather patterns. If the whips are harvested during the dormant months, not only will the plant be happier and growth be stronger the following season, but the withies will contain less moisture and not be as likely to crack when bent. Reduced moisture content also makes the willow easier to store, with less shrinkage and shorter drying time. Over the years I have tried many methods of harvesting, but I always come back to a sharp knife or secateurs. They provide the cleanest cut, thereby reducing the risk of disease entering a jagged wound. When cutting, it is good practice to ensure that your secateurs are sharp and have been disinfected. If using a knife, cut on the diagonal in an upward direction, rather than cutting down into the stool. I find the upright osiers easier to cut through if you bend them slightly towards the "back" side of the withy while making the cut on the "belly" side.

Harvest on a dry day, when the willow has seen no rain. If the willow is slightly damp the bundles will hold water, and that will cause mould and rot, making your willow only fit for compost or kindling. If leaves are on the rods when bundled, they will encourage damaging mould and deteriorate the willow quality when stored.

Withies could be used immediately but will be easier to work with and offer less shrinkage if left for a couple of weeks after cutting. When working with "green" willow, you will find significant shrinkage as the willow dries. The withies may become a third thinner than when cut, so weaving must be very tight to compensate. I really enjoy working with "green" willow. The bark colours are vibrant, plant energy is strong, and I don't have to soak it or work with wet hands.

Cut as close to the origin of the withy as possible.

When cutting with a blade, cut diagonally in an upward direction while bending the withy backwards.

Each year multiple rods will grow from the crown of the plant.

Sorting and storing

As I harvest my willow, I keep the varieties separate and place butts at one end of the pile and tips at the other. This first step in sorting makes all subsequent steps straightforward.

If you are intending to use your willow for living willow structures, there is no need to stand it in water, unless you won't use it before it dries out.

Grade the osiers into sizes, for ease of storage but also to make it easier when it comes to retrieving materials from your bolts. I have found the quickest way to grade the withies is to place them butt down in a tub, beside marks on the wall which represent height. Standing on a stool, begin pulling out the tallest tips. Repeat the process, descending in size, resulting in handsome bundles of graded osiers, beautifully tied with a "Somerset Rose" (see Chapter 4, "Basic Techniques") and calling out to be played with.

As you sort your withies, you will find yourself with a load of off-cuts. Your trimmings can be planted to make more plants.

Freshly cut golden willow and red dogwood, bundled and tied with twisted withies.

If your bolts have been harvested and sorted while dry, they can be stored in an airy place, out of direct sunlight, and preferably standing on their butts. If they must be kept horizontally, ensure there is some air flow underneath. The willow will dry and shrink (you may find the bundles become loose and need retying) and keep well for years, allowing you to take what you need, as required.

Your willow may not need soaking until the May after cutting, but this will be sooner if weather conditions are hot. The withies

Pull the tallest tips to grade in size.

will stay bendy until they dry. Following that, the willow will need to be soaked to achieve the flexibility required for weaving. Soaking times differ according to the type of willow you are using. Willow with no bark (such as stripped white or buff willows) will require one hour per 30 cm (1 foot). Willow with bark on will require one day per 30 cm (1 foot). Although I prefer working with fresh willow, using pre-dried and soaked willow does offer benefits. There is less shrinkage to contend with and the willow becomes "kinder", with less springiness, meaning you may achieve a tighter and more even weave.

If time is pressing and willow soaking times need to be reduced, you can soak in heated water, although the heat may darken the bark colour.

A cattle trough provides an ideal soaking tank. The barn (built using locally sourced timber extracted with horses and milled using a wood-powered steam engine) collects rainwater, which is channelled from the roof into the 1,000-litre water container and fed by hose into the soaking tank.

Hedges

Hedges often offer a wide variety of withies, as well as other shoots that can be utilised for crafts. However, before you start snipping away, do bear in mind that in Britain these days everything belongs to someone. (Booo! Give us back our common land!) As removing cuttings from someone's property may be seen as criminal damage, you may like to approach the owner for permission first. Before I grew my own willow, I depended entirely on cuttings from hedgerows, gardens, and utility land – and a very wide variety there is, too! One year I managed to find 18 different colours growing within trotting distance of my camp. I have not yet met a landowner who minded me taking cuttings from their hedges before they were flailed,* after realising that my cutting method would not leave any gaps or introduce disease to the hedgerow plants. There are many plants apart from willow that offer flexible one-year shoots suitable for weaving. If a stick will bend around your wrist without breaking, then you will be able to weave with it.

Traditionally, hedges should be managed between November and March. I would go further and suggest that hedges should only be cut from December to February inclusive, as we must start taking more care of our feathered friends. Widespread hedgerows in Britain are a consequence of extensive (and on-going) enclosure acts (when people are excluded from their land by governments) and as such are fairly recent. However, hedges have become crucial habitat

> **Hedge flailing.* Most British hedges are "flailed" these days, which is the process of cutting vegetation with heavy-duty blades, attached to a rotating mechanical drum. It is seen to be fast and effective and promoting slower growth, but it has a hugely detrimental effect on the health of the hedge, the purpose of the hedge, and the environmental benefits of the hedge.
>
> The large spinning blades tear the plant apart, causing gaping wounds that allow disease to enter the plant, often leaving large gaps in hedges. Those gaps, combined with the repeated cutting of the plant at the same point, high off the ground, result in hedges that are not fit for purpose. Their traditional purpose is to contain livestock. Good practice used to recommend that hedges were flailed in three-year rotation, ensuring that all farms had areas that provided habitat, food, and breeding sites for birds and insects, as many creatures rely on hedgerow shoots that are older than one year. It now appears to be widespread agricultural practice to cut hedges back as hard and as often as possible, with the Department for Environment and Rural Affairs (DEFRA) frequently giving farmers permission to cut during the bird-breeding season, despite a loss of over 80% of many of our small, hedge-nesting birds during the last fifty years. A traditionally managed hedge, by contrast, supplies resources such as fuel, food, medicine, skilled employment for people, and habitat, food, and breeding opportunities for many of our endangered species.

This traditionally laid hedge provides wildlife with cool shade during summer heat and respite from the elements in winter. The dense layering of branches offers small creatures protection from predation. The seven-or-so-year cycle of laying allows an abundance of nuts, seeds, berries, medicinal herbs, craft materials, and fuel for heating.

Same plants and growing conditions as the previously pictured laid hedge, but this hedge is flailed annually and provides little habitat, breeding opportunities, or food for wildlife and no useful resource for people.

in that they provide a small alternative to some of our extensive woodland loss (primarily due to wars and industry). A hedge is a strip of woodland and is habitat for many living things that have been left with few other places to go, so please be careful, gentle, and empathic when harvesting from a hedge. Even in the winter a healthy hedge contains much life, including hibernating creatures such as dormice. The diversity our living country boundaries offer should be treasured, nurtured, and fully appreciated. In this time of enormous pressures on our flora and fauna, the greenwood rows are crucial bastions of wildlife.

Gardens

Another good source of cuttings can be gardens, where ornamental willows are included to provide winter colour. Have a chat with the owner: quite often this can be a "win–win" situation; you get the waste materials for making things, and they get a free, knowledgeable pruner and maybe even something lovely made from their own garden. Disinfect your secateurs before and after entering someone's garden, to minimise the risk of spreading disease. Ensure your secateurs are sharp and that your cuts are clean and preferably on the diagonal. Bear in mind the shape of the plant that you are leaving behind after pruning. Some plants would rather not be pruned in the winter, so do check before slicing. Cuttings can be used and stored in the same way as described above in "Sorting and Storing".

Willow merchants

If you are not able to grow or gather your own materials, then you may like to buy from a willow merchant.

Willow used to be sold in "bolts" – withies sorted and sold in lengths, but with a standard measurement (just over 3 feet) around the circumference of the bundle's base. Now I only know of willow being sold by the kilo. Withy merchants may offer mixed bundles, which are useful for home artisans as most projects require a variety of length and thickness. If the provenance of your materials matters to you, check that the willow is grown in your locality, or at least your country, and in a way that is environmentally considerate.

Although varieties offered have expanded in recent decades, the main species available from withy merchants is *S. triandra* "Black Maul". Black Maul is the osier traditionally grown for basketry, as it has a regular habit of growing tall, slender withies, with no side shoots. Black Maul is prepared in a number of ways and sold as distinct types:

- "Greens" are freshly cut withies that have not yet dried out and do not require soaking prior to use.
- "Browns" are the "greens" that have dried.
- "Buff" have been boiled in their bark and then stripped, revealing the inner withy, which has been dyed by the barks' tannins during the boiling process.
- "Steamed" have been steamed, the heat causing the bark to turn a very dark brown, almost black in some cases.
- "Whites" have been harvested in the winter, bundled up, and then stood, butt down, in a few inches of water, so the stick remains alive. At the beginning of spring the withy begins to draw up water, and the bark becomes easy to peel. Each stick is stripped of bark, so revealing the white interior.

Contrasting with the vibrant colours of freshly cut willow are "whites" and "steamed" from the nearby Somerset Levels.

Small-scale producers are now a rarity on the Somerset Levels, but within living memory the industry had thrived. Willow harvesting and processing relied on the help of transient seasonal workers from all over the country.

Prior to the loud, scary, mechanical bark strippers, which can be run from the back of a tractor, withies were drawn through a metal brace, an item shaped like a giant inverted old-fashioned clothes peg. Each buff and white stick was stripped by hand, which was generally the role of women and children. On one memorable occasion, when selling my willow wares on the side of the road, an octogenarian lady approached me with a twinkle in her eye and proceeded to tell me all about her days as a Somerset stripper.

Preparation

Of all the willows, Black Maul is one of the kindest. For beginners, young people, or those with arthritic hands, white or buff willow in shorter, finer lengths will be easiest to use and have the shortest soaking time at one hour per 30 cm (1 foot). You could soak in the morning for use in the afternoon. On the downside, it does dry out quickly while being used, so it is imperative to keep the soaked willow wrapped in a wet cloth and take only the rods that you need at that moment.

The "greens", "browns", and "steamed" need to be soaked for one day per 30 cm (1 foot), as they have their bark on. Willows should be fully submerged in cool, clean water. I used to rely on streams and rivers to soak my willow. As the willow was free from contaminants, I felt fine about sinking it into a watercourse for a few hours, roped to a tree to stop it floating away. At times I have reclaimed my bundles to find them full of fresh-water shrimps and white-clawed crayfish: such a joy to remove those beings carefully and watch them swim free in the clear, cool water. Not so fun to find your withies coated with slurry and dead fish though, so these days I am forced to use a trough and mourn the state of the streams and rivers. Try not to over-soak your willow, as the quality will deteriorate and the withies will become all slimy.

Wrap the soaked willow in a damp shroud and leave to "mellow", allowing the bark to become less slippery and less likely to be damaged in the weaving process, while keeping the inner wood wet and flexible. I'm of a mind that willow should be mellowed for the same amount of time as soaking, but I don't know why I think that, and anyway a few hours is usually enough. Try it out and see what works for you. Keep all soaked willow under a damp cloth until the moment you weave with it. You may like to have a water spray bottle to hand if your working conditions are very dry.

Try not to keep willow wet for days on end, as it will deteriorate, become mouldy, and rot. If you find yourself with surplus to requirements, you can dry the excess by spreading in a well-ventilated area. It will need to dry fairly quickly, or it will grow mould, but fully dehydrated it can be stored again. Every time you soak and dry your willow, its quality will diminish.

"White Willow Unicorn" (c. 2004).

4

Basic techniques

This chapter includes information about terms and techniques needed for the sculpture projects described in following chapters. Read through before you embark upon your willow work, to familiarise yourself with terminology and methodology, and then use as a reference point when required.

The anatomy of willow

Willow has such versatility and its own character as a living being ... each stick is unique, but patterns unite them.

Pick up a withy and feel it in your hands, feel the way it bends – can you feel how it wants to bend one way, but resists bending the other? Most willow wands will favour bending in one direction as they reach towards the sun. You will notice that when you bend the way the willow favours, a round shape is easily created. The inside of the round is the "belly" side of the withy.

If you try to bend the willow the other way, you will find resistance – that is the "back" and, like our spine, it is not too keen on bending backwards. It is important to know the back and the belly, as working with this natural property will help to determine the shape of your sculpture.

Other anatomical terms you will use are "tip" and "butt". The tip is the thin end at the top of the plant growth, the butt is the thicker end of the rod, which has been cut from the "stool".

Willow ties and wraps

Personally I strongly disapprove of using anything other than natural, biodegradable materials for ties on willow sculpture. Willow ties and wraps are consistent with the underlying ecological principles of willow sculpture, do not become damaging human detritus, look better, display the maker's skill, and, with living willow, avoid the real danger of garrotting the plant.

Twisting the withy

Wraps and ties need highly flexible withies, almost rope-like. By lightly twisting the length before binding, the longitudinal fibres that make up the stem are loosened, and the willow will bend without kinking. Hold the butt of the withy in your non-dominant hand and, with your dominant hand, work your way up towards the tip, twisting a little as you go. It may take a little practice to get the feel of it. Stop twisting before you hear the willow crack, which would indicate that the internal willow fibres have separated.

Self-holding tie

This is a quick and easy method of tightly binding two or more withies together. For the tie you will require one withy that is long, regular, and very slender.

First, twist the withy as described before. With your non-dominant hand grasp the butt end of the withy firmly lengthways against the bundle that you are tying and bend it at a right angle, beginning to wrap around the area to be tied and including the withy's own butt. Keep the turns tight around the

pieces to be tied, ending by securing the tip. The tip can be secured by weaving in, or knotting, or cramming into a gap. This tie can be large or small. The thickness of willow used for the bind should be representative of the size of the willow it is tying.

Cross tie

Cross ties are useful when tying two withies at right angles to each other. Start by holding crossed withies in your non-dominant hand, along with the butt end of a third withy, a long, very fine, flexible weaver. Begin to tie the weaver tight around the crossed stick, taking the willow behind and in front of all of the rods to hold them in place. When you get near the end of your weaver, tuck the tip into the cross tie and pull tight.

The completed cross tie

Binding wraps

Binding wraps are a method of effectively and beautifully gathering multiple sticks together and are based on a wrapped cross-handle in basketry. The technique is useful when binding leg sticks together, making antlers, or at other times when you'd like to bind rods together giving an ordered, decorative effect.

For the wrap, you will require multiple equal-sized withies that are long, regular, and very slender.

First, give each of these withies a twist.

Take the butt ends of all of the withies and ensure they are well anchored, before wrapping them around the part you are binding. I generally work all of the wrapping withies together, but to start with you may find one at a time easier to manage.

Ensure the wrapping weavers are sitting snugly parallel to each other. Ease the group round, supporting them as they turn and keeping them as tight as possible to the part they are wrapping. When you get to the tips allow yourself a good 6 inches (15 cm) to effectively tie the tips in.

If soaked willow is used and dries as a wrap, it sets in place and will retain its shape when removed from the central core, which is useful for creating effects such as long, ringletted hair.

Somerset Rose

A "Somerset Rose" is a traditional willow bind, used since time immemorial. When I began visiting the Somerset Levels in the early 1990s, that method of tying was standard among willow growers. At some point all seems to have become plastic, and the once widespread skill of binding with willow is dropping out of existence. To see a life-long withy grower bind a bolt with a Somerset Rose is an action of flowing beauty. That simple act represents a symbiotic relationship between people and their surroundings, which stretches into prehistory. I favour tying with a Rose, but haven't got anywhere close to the fluidity and swiftness of movement that I witnessed on the Levels.

For the tie, you will require one withy, which is long, regular, and slender.

Twist the withy along the length, taking particular care with the top 18 inches (45 cm). When the experts twist the willow for ties, they stand on the tip end and spin the butt end round, like cranking a vintage car to start the engine – give it a go, it's great when it works! About 30 cm (1 foot) from the tip, bend the withy, creating a loop at the top, roughly the length of half a thumb. Twist the thin part of the withy around the thicker part, three times in a downward direction and three times back up, keeping it tight all the while. Take the tip through the loop twice to prevent unravelling.

Stand with the bundle in front of you, side on, and slide the butt end of the weaver under the bundle away from you. Bring the butt up and over, towards you, and thread it through the loop. Push the loop tight against the bundle (you may like to use your foot) while bearing pressure on the butt end until you have pulled the bundle tight. Give the butt end of the tying withy a further twist at the point it is passing through the loop as you bend it back on itself and then continue to twist the butt end. Twist three times, then pass around its own bend, twist three times more and round again, a further three, and once more round, then bring the butt down towards the base of the bundle. Twist again and then insert, in an upward direction, behind the Rose, pushing up into the bundle until there is a loop 10–12 cm (4–5 inches) below the Rose, which is twisted again to hold it all in place.

Something about this act feels like a magic spell . . . keep trying it and see what you think!

I honour this knot by including it in many of my sculptures, particularly in the wild willow women, who may have a Somerset Rose for their lips.

Willow sculpture techniques

Snowshoe

A basic shape that forms the foundation of many willow sculptures is the snowshoe. In this book it forms the beginning of the willow pig project, with the curved end representing the rump. In animals with a leaner shape, such as a deer, a horse, or a lurcher, you would turn the initial, vertical snowshoe, so that the curved end represented the chest cavity.

For the snowshoe you will require one withy that is long and regular; in terms of size, consider the "general rule of thumb" (GRT):

that is, beginning the sculpture process with thick willow rods, and decreasing the willow size gradually as the sculpture progresses.

Take the withy in both hands and gently rock it while creating a curve halfway along. Bring the ends of the willow slowly towards you as you are rocking the stick. This action is loosening the fibres inside the stem, enabling easier bending without kinking. Cross the butt and tip ends of the weaver in front of you, making the shape smaller by moving the crossing point further up the butt side of the shape, allowing plenty of the tip end to remain free for use as a tie. When you have the correct size, use the tip end to secure the crossing point, using a figure of eight or a crossing knot, and then tucking the remaining tip tightly away.

Anchoring

Many weaving and tying processes are made easier if the butt end is properly anchored. Anchoring is simply pushing the thick end of the willow into a gap tight enough to hold it firmly in place. Find a gap to push the butt into that will provide grip by the opposing pressure of existing weavers, pinching new addition(s) in place, so preventing slippage. If there is no existing anchoring point, then the butt end may have to be held in place by incorporating into a wrap or a tie. Another option, if one can't find pinching gaps, is to bend the butt end over to create a "hook". The withy can then be inserted and pulled back so that the hook holds.

Weaving

To weave is the action of repeatedly going in and out, to and fro, behind and in-front of stouter sticks. Alternated weaving, or a pinching weave, creates an opposing pressure that holds everything in place. A feature of fine basketry work is the regularity of weave, and indeed, basketry is generally extremely formulaic. Not so with willow sculpture, which offers the opportunity for many free-flowing styles and effects. However, in order to create strength, a certain amount of weaving is required.

In willow sculpture I have generally found that ease of weave requires the butt end of the willow to be used first. As with a needle when you sew, the butt end is repeatedly passed behind and in front, for over a third of the withy's length. When the weaver(s) is anchored, attention can be turned to the tip end, which is far more amenable to being woven into smaller gaps.

I am often struck by the similarities between willow work and textiles, the stake and strand of basketry being so like the warp and weft of cloth. I often choose to represent the attire of my willow figures using willow weaves that emulate textile techniques, contrasting with the three-strand willow sculpture technique I use to create muscle form, as can be seen in projects and examples throughout this book.

Random weave

Random weave is the technique used for covering the shell of the sculpture by weaving one withy at a time in various directions. As you construct your sculpture, you will be making the gaps between your willow smaller, while creating the compact shape that you desire. Work around the sculpture, ensuring even distribution, and dissecting each big gap in turn with your next weaver. Before you insert the butt end, think about where the withy will be placed. Work with the will of the willow: be firm, but don't try to fight it. When working on a large sculpture, I like to put piles of graded withies at various points around the body and move from area to area, for consistent coverage. My non-growing sculptures are usually very densely woven, as a stylistic choice, and I use the random weave as a foundation, leaving enough space for an intricate three-strand finish.

Three-strand technique

The three-strand technique was a style I developed in response to feeling that the random weave alone was failing to enhance the gentle undulations, anatomy, and physiology of the willow sculptures.

The finish is what makes a sculpture, a subjective process that demonstrates your uniqueness as a maker. For me, when the lines of the willow go in all directions, it's a bit chaotic on the eye, whereas the three-strand technique brings some aesthetic order and allows emphasis to define parts of the creation. Of course, it doesn't have to be three rods – you could use two rods, four, five, or more, but the basic principle remains: by working multiple rods together, you create a cohesiveness that would not otherwise be.

I have always been drawn to use three: one for the maiden, one for the mother, and one for the crone. Willow taught me this with her feminine energy, although the number three is held as special by many ancient cultures.

Weavers should be of equal length and diameter. Tap the butts together and trim them on the diagonal. Trim the tips so the rods are neat and tidy. As with the other weaves, lead with the butts. Progressively layer the woven willow, following the GRT.

"Light" (c. 2004).

Making ears

When making an animal, the ears bring the creature alive. Animals' ears are extremely expressive and worth paying attention to. The technique that I have developed for making ears requires one flexible medium-sized withy per ear, and many very fine weavers for infill. By using one continuous withy for the structure, the ear is well anchored into the body. The design I'm about to describe can be altered to make many sizes and shapes, but the procedure remains the same. It's worth looking at pictures of the animal you are making to assess where exactly their ears sit in relation to the rest of their head. Each ear is made the same way.

The butt end of the structural withy is slyped (cut on the diagonal) and pushed straight down into the head, starting on the side of the ear that is closest to the middle of the head, ensuring it is anchored. When that stick is firmly in place, use your thumbnail to kink it at the required height. Bring the tip end of the withy down towards the side of the head and insert, level with the original insert but pointing backwards and diagonally upwards, so the tip emerges behind the triangle you have formed. Keep the willow curved to create a rounded shape to the lobe of the ear. Take the tip up to the kink at the top of the ear, and secure in place with a willow tie.

To keep the shell-like quality of the ear, only the back two sides will be woven. Weave from the base upwards from side to side, wrapping around the outer edge sticks as you turn. You will notice that on every other return you will have to wrap around the back stick to keep the hollow depth of the ear.

Basketry techniques

Basketry is a very different discipline from willow sculpture, despite sharing similarities and having overlaps. Learning basketry will likely benefit your developing sculpture techniques, and some of the established weaves of basketry are essential tools in willow sculpture. The following are a few basketry techniques that I regularly use in sculpture.

Pairing

Pairing is a pinching weave, used to hold uprights in place. A pair of weavers is used. Each weaver starts behind consecutive uprights.

BASIC TECHNIQUES

Traditionally woven from left to right, with the left hand supporting while the right hand performs the weaving, left weaver jumping over the right, behind the next upright and forward through the next gap. Left-handed people may find this weave easier working from right to left.

Laid-in join

Laid-in joins must be the simplest approach to continuing a weave when you have run out of withy. Lay a new weaver directly on top of the one that needs replacing and carry on! There are many types of joins in basketry, but willow sculpture is less prescriptive.

Slype

A slype is a quick diagonal cut at the base of a withy, which allows it be easily inserted into a gap, or to sit flush against a weave. Hold the withy under your non-dominant arm, with the butt heading forward in front of you, angled from the elbow, down from horizontal. With your knife in your dominant hand, slice diagonally across the withy, directing the knife away from your body. With practice you will find that there is a particular angle of cut that makes your slice easy and safe. For me, a traditional slype has always been a three-movement, craft-knife practice, with a cut made downwards followed by one from each side to create a point, but you can cut a diagonal with secateurs to the same purpose.

Woodwork

Whittling

When I was a kid, it was said that one should never be without a piece of string, a knife, and a five-penny piece. Well, a five-penny piece (for the phone box) is no good any more, a piece of string is always handy, and, when out in the wilds, I couldn't do without a sharp blade! Whittling refers to the art of shaving shapes from wood with a craft knife and can be as simple as paring a peg to fit in a hole, or as complex as a walking stick comprising highly detailed rearing horses, with flowing manes, whittled and blackened in the fire, rubbed down and oiled to give it gloss, a shiny copper two-penny piece set in the end and a trim of polished copper to finish: just like some of my clever horse-drawn travelling companions made while sitting around a summer stick fire.

It is important you have a knife that fits into your hand, and that it is your own knife, imbibed with your personal creative energy. I recommend you invest in one with a good-quality blade, which folds closed when not in use and has a blade-locking feature when open. Always whittle away from your body – NEVER towards you or using your leg as a support. Be careful of the tip of your knife around your fingers, hands, and the fleshy mound of your thumb.

Round wood mortise and tenon

I do not claim to be a joiner, by any stretch of the imagination, but I do favour joining wood with only natural materials, and this joint is ideal for the right angles made by wooden frames. Whittle down one stick (the tenon), insert into a drilled hole (the mortise) in the other, and then hold in place with a withy "peg": a small hole is drilled through the mortise and tenon and the withy peg inserted, which is then woven around the joint for further reinforcement. This join can be scaled up for larger sculptures.

Nailed / screwed joints

Probably quicker and requiring less skill, joints held with nails or screws are an option. You would be well advised to whittle shallow notches into the round wood poles where they adjoin, so they sit comfortably together. To prevent the wood splitting, make a pilot hole with a drill bit slightly smaller than the diameter of screw / nail you will use. If using nails, use annular ring shanks, which have ridges along the shaft to hold them firm. Do be careful not to leave sharp points of screws or nails exposed: they will catch your hands while you are weaving and cause injury.

Plinths

In the early days of making willow geese I would stand them in the ground, which is all very well as long as you have ground to stick them in, a spike to pre-make the leg holes, are happy to leave them in one place, and don't mind the legs rotting quickly. A plinth is

an obvious alternative and can add dimension to your sculpture by providing a complementary effect. My methods of attachment have always remained predictably simple: just drilling holes in the wood in which to insert the legs. Very occasionally I have been known to incorporate a piece of 6-mm metal rod (or a 5-inch nail) for extra support, and wrapping around the metal with willow. If your plinth is for an inside sculpture, you may wish to glue felt to the bottom, to prevent scratches on furniture.

Preserving

How long a non-growing willow sculpture lasts will largely depend on where it is kept and how it is treated, although the method of construction and density of weave will also influence longevity.

If your sculpture is kept in dry conditions, it will last indefinitely; if it is kept in damp boggy woods, with no protection, it will only last a couple of years.

Although I have previously used chemical preservatives, I no longer do so, and so cannot recommend them. As well as the obvious problems linked to handling toxic agents, my sculptures often become home to various insects, birds, and small mammals. For outside sculptures I use a high-specification, non-toxic oil preparation, which offers ultraviolet protection, waterproofing, and antifungal properties. Outside sculptures should initially be treated straight after being made, once they are fully dry. Following treatment, beads of moisture will collect on the sculpture when it rains, instead of being absorbed. Repeat oil treatment as necessary.

I have one particular sculpture that has been put out for the last 15 summers and brought in for the winters, is fairly regularly oiled, and is still going strong, as well as being a favoured location for a robin's nest (where the sculpture's heart would be).

With basketry made from fresh materials, I apply a few coats of Danish oil to the "green" willow after weaving. Danish oil is non-toxic and suitable for kitchen-surface use. I have found that the oil enhances and preserves the natural bark colours as the basket ages.

5

Weaving a willow goose

So, willow sculpture! When hosting workshops, I guide attendees through the process step by step, increasing knowledge and skill by practical application. One of the first animals that I developed a pattern for was the goose, but the same basic formation can be used for many birds, including hens and cockerels, swans, peacocks, and herons.

We shall begin by making a goose: 100% willow – no wire, no plastic, no tape or string. How appropriate it seems, when sculpting with willow, to start with an animal that loves to paddle in the water!

This goose can be made using fresh willow or pre-dried and soaked willow. With pre-dried you can achieve a tighter and more formal effect. The goose can be stuck in the ground or set on a plinth. If using fresh willow, you have the option of leaving the legs 10 inches too long and planting it to become a living willow sculpture (more on this in Chapter 9, "Weaving a Living Willow Sculpture"). If you are intending to make this goose to grow, you will probably want to use fewer, slightly thicker fresh rods, leaving the finish with enough gaps to allow room for new growth.

All amounts and dimensions listed in the project recipes are approximate. When working with natural materials, I embrace that no two pieces are the same, and the wilder the wood you are using, the more this will be the case. I invite you to relax and welcome the variability of numbers!

When constructing willow sculpture, you will begin with your thickest rods and gradually decrease the size with which you are working as the sculpture develops. As you progress through the sculpture, your willow requirements will gradually get thinner and thinner – the GRT that underpins all of your willow sculptures.

While working on a three-dimensional creation, keep standing back, turning it, or walking around and examining it from all angles. Work evenly around the sculpture; whatever you do on one side, repeat on the other. If you prioritise one part for too long you run the risk of the finished sculpture appearing as if it were many sculptures stuck together.

If you get cross with it, walk away (unless you want a scary sculpture): the sculpture will absorb your emotions and mirror them back at you . . . sculpting in willow can be a journey into one's psyche!

The basic procedure is:

- make a shape;
- reinforce the shape;
- decorate the shape.

Willow goose foundations

✂ **Step 1.** Begin by gathering and preparing your materials. You will need:

- 6 withies, approximately 150 cm (5 feet) in length, about as thick as your thumb at the butt end, for the legs;
- 2 withies, approximately 150 cm (5 feet) in length, slightly thinner than the leg sticks, for the initial frame and neck;
- 1 withy, approximately 150 cm (5 feet) in length, very flexible, to create the tension strap between the tail and

the chest;
- 20 medium-thickness withies, approximately 120 cm (4 feet) in length, for continuing the framework and finishing;
- a handful of very fine, flexible weavers, approximately 90 cm (3 feet) in length, for ties and wraps;
- a small bundle of fine twigs, for the beak;
- a set of secateurs.

Step 2. Take the two withies that are slightly thinner than the leg sticks and hold them with the butts towards you and crossed – this will be the tail end of the bird. Ensure that the withies are lying with the "back" side facing outwards, and the "belly" side facing inwards. This will form the side curves of the undercarriage of the goose.

It is worth bearing in mind that the sculpture will enlarge as willow is added. First we make a strong foundation on which to build the detail – check that the frame you're building is smaller than the finished article is supposed to be.

❀ **Step 3.** Using the withy designated as a tension strap, place the butt end behind the cross, so the tip end is in the centre of the other two.

You'll notice in this picture I am holding with my left hand and weaving with my right. My dominant hand is my right hand – if you are left-handed, you may find it easier to hold with your right and weave with your left.

WEAVING A WILLOW GOOSE

✣ **Step 4.** Now we are going to tie the cross together, as tightly as possible. Keeping hold of the cross and the butt end of the tension weaver firmly with your non-dominant hand, take the willow from behind the back, over the top and under, ensuring that it pinches its own butt end in place to prevent unravelling, and then to the side, so the tie is going both horizontally and vertically as you are looking at it. For enhanced flexibility, you may wish to twist the willow prior to bending (see Chapter 4).

When you have a good firm tie, bring the tension weaver from underneath, up and over the centre of the cross – it is important to finish off in this position, because the rest of the length is going to create the top tension strap, creating a three-dimensional shape, which will form the back of the goose.

✂ **Step 5.** Brace the firmly tied tail end against your body, while crossing the withies about 45 cm (1.5 feet) away from the tail, creating an eye shape. Holding this new cross, bring it upwards, towards your body. Use the tip end of the tension weaver to tightly tie the new cross, thus creating a three-dimensional shape and the inner framework of the goose.

Step 6. During this process you will probably find that the three-dimensional shape wants to flatten itself back into a two-dimensional shape. Gently encourage it not to. We shall be reinforcing its depth in a moment.

✂ **Step 7.** Before we do that reinforcement, we are going to form the basis of the neck and head. Gather each of the protruding side rods and kink them just above the second tie, bringing them together to form the neck.

✽ **Step 8.** Remembering that this is the internal framework of the goose – the back will get higher and the undercarriage lower – work out the height of the top of the head and kink the willow so it bends at a 90° angle. If the neck is too long, it'll look like a swan; too short, and it will look like a duck. If you find that your goose's neck is a bit wonky, uneven, or at a strange angle, and the willow really wants to be there, I suggest that you embrace the direction in which the willow is taking you – these oddities often end up being the part of the sculpture that gives it a unique and defining character.

✤ **Step 9.** Kink the willow again, about 5 cm (2 inches) away from the first kink, and bend it under: this will form the foundation of the head.

Then take the remainder of those two rods and wind them down the neck and into the body. You will notice that if you take both of the sticks clockwise, the goose will look to the right. Anti-clockwise, and it will look to the left. You may want to take one of the rods down clockwise and one anticlockwise if you want the goose to look straight ahead.

✾ **Step 10.** Tie the ends off into the chest; by doing so, you will simultaneously support the three-dimensional shape by drawing the side sticks together.

✂ **Step 11.** First stage complete . . . we have just created a three-dimensional shape, using nothing but willow, our hands, and our skill . . . well done!

Now we have created the shape, procedure dictates that we reinforce the shape.

Step 12. Beginning to reinforce the three-dimensional shape, we can now stop its inclination to flatten. Remembering our GRT, that as the sculpture progresses the rods get thinner, take an appropriate rod and insert the butt end into the base of the neck somewhere – it doesn't really matter where, find a hole. If your weaving is so tight that you cannot find a hole to poke your willow through, then make a gap with a bodkin, a screw-driver, a tent peg, or whatever comes to hand. Once the butt end is anchored in, take the rest of the withy and take it diagonally around the body of the goose – you can kink it where you want it to stay, if that will help. When you get to the tip, use it as a tie to hold itself in place (see Chapter 4).

❀ **Step 13.** When you have completed that action, repeat it symmetrically – put the butt into the base of the neck and take it in the opposite direction around the body. Even after just adding these two weavers, you will notice how much stronger the frame is becoming.

During the process of making a sculpture you may find that things slip around: at any point you can use a small piece of willow, or the end of a close-by weaver, to tie those naughty pieces in place. Personally, I use nothing other than willow as a tie.

❀ **Step 14.** Although the basic shape of a goose is now recognisable, you will see that the body requires more depth – geese have a great deal of fatty tissue upon their breasts, which keeps them warm against the water, and their undercarriage is quite substantial.

Begin to build up the undercarriage of the goose by anchoring a couple of withies into the base of the neck, but from the front this time. Bend the withies under and towards the tail, making the most of the natural curve of the willow, with the "belly" creating the round chest shape. Secure the withy in place by tying around the tail; if there is surplus length to the withy, bring it back in to the body and weave through the existing withies to add strength.

❁ **Step 15.** Now we have made a shape, we need to reinforce the shape, and that is what we shall do, using one weaver at a time and "sewing" into the sculpture with the butt end of the withy. When you have woven the butt end of your weaver probably a third or a quarter of the length, it should be held tight by the weaving, and you can turn your attention to the rest of the weaver, which is easier to bend in and out as it tapers towards the tip. We are aiming to create an even latticework over the body of the bird.

Step 16. The weavers can be added in all directions, but remember to work symmetrically – that is, whatever you add on one side, be sure to add a similar (not necessarily identical) rod on the other. In order to decide where to put the next stick look at your bird and look for the biggest gap between the weaving. Dissect that gap with your weaver. Remember that you are aiming to reinforce your shape, not necessarily change it at this point, and you want an even coverage. Try to use the weavers efficiently, by weaving them along the surface of the sculpture. Weavers stuck into the middle of the goose are completely pointless (unless it is a feature of your design). End this process when you have a fairly even latticework, with gaps about 2.5 cm² (1 square inch) each, creating a strong shell. It is important not to over-weave at this point, or you will struggle adding detail later.

Adding the legs

❀ **Step 17.** Now you have created a strong shell, which has evenly woven latticework, you can add the legs. This is a good point in time to have a look at any pictures of geese that you may have for reference. Note where their legs are in relation to the rest of their body. You will probably find that they are about halfway along the undercarriage, and towards the side edges, rather than in the middle.

You have three sticks for each leg, which allows you to give the leg some shape.

Complete one side at a time:

- First, drop the middle stick, butt down, straight through the body from the top, so it emerges where the centre of the leg would emerge.
- Then insert the other two sticks through the body, at about 45° from the vertical, front and back. Underneath, the front one will emerge one lattice square forward of the central rod, and the one coming from the tail end will emerge one lattice square behind the central leg rod.

✂ **Step 18.** Lay the goose on its side and gather all of the leg sticks up in your non-dominant hand. Ensure that the legs are a few inches longer than the length you will ultimately require – you can always cut them back, but you can't add any on!

Take a long, fine, flexible weaver and insert the butt end into the underneath of the body, next to the leg. Grasp it in your non-dominant hand, with the leg sticks, so that the tip end of the weaver is extending past the "feet" of the goose.

Step 19. Take the weaver and bend it just below your non-dominant hand and tightly wrap around the bundle of rods in an upward direction, towards the body of the goose. This way the weaver is pinching itself in place, as well as holding the leg rods together.

When you reach the tip of the weaver, begin to weave it backwards and forwards between the individual leg sticks, then tuck the end into a gap and pull tight to secure.

✖ **Step 20.** The leg rods can now be slid upwards through the goose so that the leg wraps are directly under the undercarriage.

The remainder of the leg sticks must be incorporated into the sculpture and should be woven into the shell, taking care not to change the existing shape (unless there is an area that would specifically benefit from some more structural support). The direction in which you choose to weave away the protruding tip ends of the leg sticks will influence the posture of the bird: if all of your leg sticks are woven in one direction, then the leg will stick out in the other direction – for example, if you were to weave all of the rods from one leg towards the neck, the leg would stick out backwards, which would make the goose stand like a running duck! You could, of course, use this to your design advantage. However, having angled legs may complicate how you arrange the plinth. For the purposes of this exercise, we are keeping it simple and aiming to have the legs coming straight down, so distribute the tip ends of the leg sticks evenly around the body.

✤ Step 21. Repeat with the other leg, and give your bird a trim of any loose ends. This is a good time for making a cuppa, having a stretch, and referring again to your reference pictures. Hopefully you will have something that clearly resembles a goose, but when you compare it to pictures, you may think that the neck and head is underdeveloped, the back may be too low, the goose may not be wide enough, the undercarriage may need work. At this point you must look at your goose with an analytical eye.

* * *

Now we have the foundations, on to the beginning of the finishing!

Willow goose finishing

The beauty of working with willow is that by the time you have got to this point, the influence of the natural materials and the subconscious transfer of your energy will have begun to shape the individual character of the creature that you are making.

Please do not look at your work harshly. Instead, go with the flow and enjoy the experience of witnessing a creature born of twigs. Embrace the quirky developments that give your creature its character.

Step 22. With some of the medium-thickness weavers, gently make and shape any additions that you feel are necessary, using the same procedure: make the shape, reinforce the shape. I sometimes find it's helpful to think of the sculpture as a quick doodle – if you were sketching, where would you put a line? I would then hold a piece of willow in the place of that imaginary line to see if it improves the shape. Once the shape is correct, weave a few slightly thinner weavers across it to hold in place. With this goose I decided to add some thickness to the neck by placing a withy right over the top of the head, raised the back slightly, and increased the crop. Keep checking against your reference pictures.

Step 23. Make the beak by picking up a bundle of very fine twigs and laying them along the top of the head, protruding forwards (longer than the ultimate length of the beak) and backwards. Insert the butt end of a weaver into the neck, so that the tip is sticking up in the air, and ensure it is well anchored. Then use the weaver to tie the bundle of twigs tightly in place. Trim the twigs protruding from the back, but leave the front ones too long for now.

WEAVING A WILLOW GOOSE   103

✺ **Step 24.** Now we begin the fine-tuning, so take a minute to think about the anatomy of the goose, how the wings sit, the direction of the feathers, the fluff of the undercarriage – the little things that give your goose life.

Using the three-strand technique, start to cover your goose, beginning with the central core – the undercarriage, the back, the neck – think about the direction of the feathers and the movement of the sinews under the skin. When you have an even coverage, move to where the wings are; think about the direction of the feathers, but also the distinctive round curve at the front of the wing, which is so suggestive of "bird" to our pattern-recognition brains. Ensure that you continue to perform the weaving action with the finishing, or your sculpture will get baggy and shapeless.

Note: With a living willow goose or other small living sculpture, you may wish to omit the three-strand technique to allow room for the plant to grow.

Step 25. Trim it up, treat if applicable, plant it if it's living, stick it straight into the ground, or put it on a plinth. You may like to find a piece of wood with a beautiful ripple-y grain and oil it well so the willow goose looks as if it is standing in a puddle.

6

Weaving a willow pig

How strange that the name "pig" is often used as an insult, yet pigs are so popular with people. They appear to have characteristics that are often found in people – it may be that recognition which endears them to us. Over the years, I have taught many hundreds of willow workers to weave willow piggies, and, despite using the same techniques, no two have ever turned out the same.

These cute little grunters are a good place to start if you have never made a willow quadruped before, as the simple shape and process will introduce you to techniques that you can scale up and complicate at will.

There are many breeds of pigs, and they do have quite different conformations. I recommend finding a couple of pictures that you will be able to refer to during the build.

This project is made with 100% natural materials – in this case, withies harvested last winter, stored, and then soaked for use. As with all willow that has been soaked for flexibility, the withies must be prevented from drying before use. You will notice, in the step-by-step pictures throughout this chapter, that the soaked rods are wrapped in a damp cloth and covered with a tarpaulin to prevent drying by the wind. All of the prepared willow is kept under cover until use.

The basic procedure for this project remains the same as before: make a shape, reinforce the shape, decorate the shape; and GRT applies.

Willow pig foundations

✤ **Step 1.** Begin by gathering and preparing your materials. You will need:

- 16 withies, approximately 150 cm (5 feet) long, about as thick as your thumb at the butt end, for the legs; from these you may like to cut two thick sticks for the snout about 30 cm (1 foot) in length
- 3 withies, approximately 150 cm (5 feet) in length, slightly thinner than the leg sticks, for the initial frame and neck;
- 16 withies, approximately 150 cm (5 feet) in length, very flexible to create / reinforce body shape;
- 20 withies, 90–120 cm (3–4 feet) in length, for continuing the framework and finishing;
- a handful of very fine, flexible weavers, approximately 90 cm (3 feet) in length, for weaving the ears, ties, and wraps;
- a set of secateurs.

Step 2.   Put aside your thickest 16 rods for the leg sticks later. You will begin by using the slightly thinner ones and making three "snowshoes" (see Chapter 4), roughly the same size as each other. These will be the start of your pig's body, and will be internal, so don't start off with the size you hope to finish with . . . leave room for growth!

Choose one of your snowshoes for the upright centre of your hog. The butt side of the snowshoe will eventually be the spine of the pig, with the curve forming the rump and the pointy end going towards the nose.

✤ **Step 3.** Take a second snowshoe and lay it on at right angles to the first, so it is sitting horizontally, just over halfway up, and pointing in the same direction. With a very fine withy, tie the pieces together using a cross tie (see Chapter 4). Then tie the two pointy ends of the snowshoes together.

✂ **Step 4.** Repeat this action with the third snowshoe, but being below the centre this time, rather than above. To prevent your sculpture becoming lopsided this early in the production, ensure that the butt sides of the two horizontal snowshoes are on alternate sides of the pig body. Do not be tempted to cut off the protruding ends of the snowshoes, as these will form the foundation of the head and, possibly, provide you with snout sticks.

✥ Step 5.

Anchor the butt end of a weaver (remember GRT) into the neck end, and curve the willow along the back, underneath, and round the other side, weaving in and out of the tied snowshoes where you can. Gently pull this weaver tight, so it begins to reinforce the three-dimensional shape that you have created with the snowshoes. Do not pull so tight that you flatten the shape – the object here is to reinforce the three-dimensional shape you have made with the snowshoes. If the weaver wants to spring away from the body, then use the tip end of the weaver to tie on to the snowshoe frame to prevent slippage.

Now you have done that in one direction, put the butt of another weaver the same as the first one into the neck end and repeat the action going in the other direction. With just these two additions, you should have a fairly rigid three-dimensional shape. The shape you have now will determine whether you are making a lean piglet or a plump piggy.

If you are finding that the sticks are all a little too springy and slippy, then use very fine weavers, or side shoots from your willow, to hold pieces in place with cross ties (see Chapter 4).

✂ **Step 6.** Now that you have a fairly rigid shape, you can begin to weave around the body without having to anchor the withies in the neck end. Complying with GRT, begin to weave around the torso, using the butt end of your weaver like a needle, sewing in and out around the shell, until the weaver is properly anchored and the butt is tucked to the inside. Take the protruding tip end of the weaver and continue to weave. In order to build your sculpture in a balanced way, whatever you do on one side, roughly repeat on the other.

❋ **Step 7.** Continue in this manner, working in all directions, beginning with the butt of your weavers, and repeating your actions evenly on each side. Look for the biggest gap and dissect it with willow, gradually forming an even latticework shell, which will form a firm foundation for the legs and the finishing detail. Aim to have your weaving skimming the surface of the shell, so the shape becomes dense and tight. Any weavers poked into the middle are doing absolutely nothing useful.

Adding the legs

✤ **Step 8.** Take four of the leg sticks that you had put aside, under the damp cloth, before you began weaving. Cast your mind to when you started joining the snowshoes, to form the original three-dimensional shape. The first hoop was placed vertically, with the butt side being the spine, the top of the willow pig. Take a look at your latticed shell, does it still work the original way up? If not, you can turn it – but this is the last chance you'll have to decide which way up the shell of the pig is going.

✤ **Step 9.**   When you are happy with which way up the top is, lay the body of the pig on its side in front of you. We will work on a back leg first. Skimming just beneath the surface of the shell, slide one of the leg sticks, butt first, from top to bottom, towards you. This stick will be the centre of the back leg.

Take a second leg stick and insert the butt end, slightly forward of the centre of the leg, skimming through the shell weaves in a diagonal direction, to meet up with the central leg stick. What you want is for each leg stick to emerge from underneath through a different gap in your latticework.

WEAVING A WILLOW PIG 117

✺ **Step 10.** With the third back leg stick you will do something slightly different. Slide the butt end of the rod from front to back, skimming through the surface weave, to near the side of the spine. Keep pushing the butt through until you have plenty of length, sticking out of the back of the pig, to the side of where the tail would be. Carefully bend the leg stick towards you, to join with the other leg sticks in your hand, creating a smooth curve consistent with the shape of a pig's derrière.

I have found that every animal has a set of characteristics which, if present, we humans recognise instantly. This is helpful with willow sculpture, as, if you can resonate with peoples' perceptions of shapes, detail becomes less necessary. One of the shapes that people associate with a pig is the shape of a ham joint, and if you can represent the shape with curving willow, your pig will become so much more alive.

❈ **Step 11.** Hopefully you now have a back leg shape that resembles a ham, but it will be flat, and a pig's thigh muscle is not.

Take your pig body and hold it upright – you are going to insert the butt end of the fourth leg stick from the top, on the far side of the spine, coming downwards in a diagonal direction, through the bottom of the body, and joining up with its fellow back-leg sticks.

This will make an upside-down pyramid shape under the pig, which will be wrapped to create the leg. You should have each of the four legs sticks coming out of adjacent, but separate, gaps in your lattice shell, in order to enhance the muscular structure of the pig's leg.

✂ **Step 12.** Clench the four leg sticks in your non-dominant hand. Take a long, fine, flexible weaver and push the butt end through your fist and up into the body of the pig. You should now have the four leg sticks and the weaver held securely in one hand, with the tip of the weaver pointing away from the body of the pig. You will now perform a self-holding tie (see Chapter 4) by wrapping the weaver tightly up the leg, towards the body, so it is binding its own butt end together with the leg sticks.

WEAVING A WILLOW PIG   121

✄ **Step 13.**   Make the wrap as tight as possible and, when you reach the tip, secure the end with a figure of eight, or knot, around the leg sticks. Ensure the wrap is not too far down the leg, as we will be trimming off the ends of the leg sticks later. If your wrap is a bit on the low side, you should be able to push all of the leg sticks up through the body at this point.

✤ **Step 14.** You will now have four bound leg sticks, creating one back leg, emerging from the underneath, and four withies sticking out of the top. We must weave the protruding ends of the leg sticks into the body, and this is a good opportunity to use those thick sticks to add to any part of the pig that is deficient of weave. Begin to add to the front, head area of the pig. You can use these sturdy sticks to create lines that are consistent with the anatomy of the pig. Shown here, the front leg stick is curved towards the rump, in order to emphasise the "ham" shape.

It is important that, as you weave in the four leg-stick tips, each of the sticks is going in a different direction, as this will stabilise the leg. If all of your leg sticks are fed forwards, then your pig leg will kick out backwards. Try to hold the leg in place as you weave away the tip ends.

Step 15.
Next we add a front leg on the same side as the rear leg you have just constructed.

The gathering of the pointy end of the snowshoes will be the shoulder area, with protruding snowshoe ends hopefully being long enough to eventually create a snout (don't worry if they are not quite that long, as we will add other snout sticks later if the ones you have are unsuitable). As with the back leg, begin by inserting a leg stick, butt end first, from top to bottom, placed at the centre of where the leg will be, and just skimming the surface of the weaving, so it is held in place on the outside of the sculpture body. The two next leg sticks will be pushed in, again just skimming

through the surface weave, on the diagonal, so the butts join the butt of the centre leg stick. The fourth rod, which adds dimension, is inserted from the top from the other side, going through the centre of the body and emerging underneath, so it can join the other leg rods.

As with the other legs, each leg rod should be emerging underneath from different gaps in your latticework willow shell, in order to assist the making of a three-dimensional muscle shape. When your four rods are in place, bind them to match the rear leg.

✂ **Step 16.** Weave the protruding tip ends of the front leg rods around the body of your sculpture, accentuating anatomical shoulder shapes and taking the weavers in all directions to ensure the leg stays straight. Begin to build the head area by taking some weavers around the protruding snowshoe ends – but not too tightly, as you will presently need to leave some room for reinforcing the head shape.

✤ **Step 17.** Now lay the piggy on its other side, and repeat the leg process of inserting rods, binding, and weaving the tip ends away, distributing the weavers evenly over the body, and beginning to build up the head end.

❋ **Step 18.** With your secateurs, trim the feet ends of the legs, so you can stand your sculpture for the remainder of the process. Be sure to leave your pig's legs a little on the long side for now. You can properly trim them when you have finished. You can always cut more off, but you won't be able to put some back on.

Willow pig finishing

What you should be looking at now is a pig-shaped sculpture that will stand up and provide a firm foundation for the finishing bits and pieces, which will likely be building up the head, jawbone, and snout, deepening the chest, adding ears and a tail, and weaving in some finer willow to create a finished look. If your piggy happens to be standing, but on three legs, that is fine – you will have an active pig, dancing a jig.

Try not to be critical of your work so far: each piggy takes on its own character, and when you have been focusing on your creation so intensely for a long time, it's easy to see only the bits you are not happy with, rather than embracing your creation as a whole. Keep at it, and enjoy the process. If you are getting frustrated, now is a good time to have a break and return later with a fresh eye.

As we embark upon the next stages, remember the GRT – we have finished weaving with our thickest willow. We may use some medium pieces for structure (adding to the undercarriage, defining the pig's cheeks, structuring the ears and tail), but most of the withies we will be using from now on will be fine weavers, as we have made and reinforced the shape. Now we are just decorating.

✂ **Step 19.**   Let's begin by working on the head: We require a smooth line from the belly to the snout, so turn your pig upside down, and take a few medium-sized weavers. Slype the ends to a point and skim through the weave of the belly, from back to front, with the butt ends.

Push the butt-end willow right through to the snout and weave the tip ends, which are protruding from the rear end, into the body.

✂ **Step 20.** Work on the jaw line (which is very strong in pigs) by using medium-thickness willow to create the shape and then reinforcing with finer weavers, to create a lattice – just as you did on the main body, but on a smaller scale. You are aiming to create a latticework that represents the shape of the head and has tight enough gaps to hold willow in place, but not so tight that you can't fit any other withies in. Turn your attention to the snout. You may have the butt ends of the original snowshoes sticking out; from these you may be able to select two that will act as the nostrils. If you don't, or if you do but they are not suitable, then take a couple of thick cuttings left from trimming your leg sticks, slype one end of each of them, and jam into the front of your piggy, so they are lodged well in place and extending further than the end of the pig's snout – they will be trimmed later.

❀ **Step 21.** When you have your nostril sticks in place, take a long, fine, flexible weaver and insert the butt end of it into the head of the pig, so the rest of the weaver is pointing forward and ready to use to secure the nostrils in place. Begin by bending the weaver as a figure of eight around the two sticks. This action allows the nostril sticks to be held at just the right distance away from each other. When you have competed a couple of figure of eights, you will then be able to take the weaver around the whole snout, without losing the spacing of the nostrils.

Step 22. Time to add the ears, which I always find such an exciting bit, as the sculpture comes to life. Ears are so expressive in animals! Here we will do a prick-eared pig, rather than a lop-eared pig. You can use the same ear-weaving method for both, but for lop-eared pigs you'd fold down the ear after weaving the base of it in place. Take two medium-sized weavers and slype the butt ends of them. Insert the slypes forward of the front legs, into the top of the head, just off-centre, and have each withy leaning out sideways.

✂ **Step 23.** Kink each ear down at the required height and push the tips into the lower cheek area, so the tips are heading through the body, weaving in an upward direction, slightly diagonally towards the rear, so it emerges behind the centre of the ear. Bring it up towards the point of the ear, and tie them together.

❀ **Step 24.** With fine weavers, fill the back two sides of the ear, leaving the front part open so your pig can hear. For more details about making ears, see Chapter 4.

Step 25. Turn your pig around, and let's give the wee fellow a tail. Take three medium weavers, slype them, and insert the first one, butt first, along the spine of the sculpture, just skimming under the surface of the weave and ensuring it becomes well anchored in place. Treat the other two tail weavers in the same manner but anchoring them in diagonally, so that as they stick out, they create a triangular shape representative of the animal's "waggy tail" muscle.

✽ **Step 26.**   There are many ways to do a tail. The simplest I have found is to grasp all three anchored tail rods, curve them in your fist, and then use one of those three to wrap up and down the tail, holding them all together in a curve. You will have to twist the wrapping weaver first (see Chapter 4).

When you have secured the wrapping weaver, the excess tail weavers can be trimmed. You may like to fray the tail willows by cutting the ends of the tail willow along the grain and separating the fibres. You may like to make the tail by plaiting the three rods, or to recreate a piggy's curly tail by pre-forming the willow with a binding wrap (see Chapter 4). It's this sort of detail that will become your maker's signature.

❋ **Step 27.** You have a pig! You may choose to leave the piggy as it is now, with a random weave, or you could seek a more ordered style and continue with a multi-rod technique, such as the three-strand technique (see Chapter 4). Use the three-strand technique to aesthetic advantage by curving the coverage to represent lines of the pig, such as the obvious muscle groups, the shoulders, and the shape of the belly.

➤ "Pig" (2023).

7

Weaving a willow stag on a hedgerow frame

An independent frame may be necessary for some sculptures, depending on their shape. Sculptures that have most of their weight in the air, such as a standing quadruped, will benefit enormously from a sturdy internal skeleton. An internal frame not only provides support for the fine willow weavers, allowing for easier repairs, but it also makes fixing to the ground easier, enables the sculpture to be moved around with less risk of damage as the willow becomes brittle, and will increase the life span of the sculpture.

Our small goose and pig projects contain a frame of sorts, in that the initial, thicker withies were used to create a frame-like shell on which to build. For this project, we will be making an independent frame with hedgerow materials – coppiced hazel, cut from a traditionally laid hedge.

A traditionally laid hedge is something that we do not see enough of since the widespread use of mechanical flail hedge cutters. A well-laid hedge provides dense cover and protection for breeding birds and mammals, as well as much rotting organic matter for the benefit of insects and fungi. For small creatures, hedges offer warmth in the winter and shade in the summer; for wildlife and us, they give food and medicine, as well as providing a plethora of craft materials and fuel for cooking and heating, compared to an annually flailed hedge,

◀ *"White Willow Stag" (c. 2005).* Constructed on a frame of fallen chestnut branches.

Make a clean cut, on the diagonal, while the plant is dormant.

which has no berries (most hedgerow plants produce fruit only on stems older than one year), no dense cover (the plants produce crowns of growth high up, where the cutting takes place, rather than at the base), and large gaps in growth, where the unclean cuts have allowed disease to enter the plants and killed off sections of the supposedly stock-proof barrier. I cannot see mechanical flailing as land husbandry, but only as a modern, destructive shortcut.

I lay my hedges on a seven-or-so-year cycle, and I see those linear strips of woodland as a crucial resource. The upward growth has the characteristics of coppice, providing multiple straight rods for use and occasional wonky ones for special features. Many kinds of wood can be coppiced. For this project we will be using hazel rods for the frame and coppiced willow that has dried, so it will need to be soaked for flexibility.

As with willow, hazel should be cut when the sap is down and the leaves are off. Cutting wood while it is dormant is more considerate to the plant, which will take fewer years to recover from its surgery and provide a material that will offer less shrinkage as it dries. Another slightly less obvious consideration may be planetary. Traditional woods-people often work with the phases of the moon when cutting timber depending on their requirements, the understanding being that when the moon is full, or new, the timber will have a higher water content, as the circulating orb draws water towards her – think of the tides of the oceans. As the moon rotates around our

Gaia, a gravitational force is exerted on the oceans, creating a bulge of water on the nearest and furthest sides of the Earth. As we living beings are full of water, it is no surprise that we may also notice an influence, and this is the same for our plant allies.

The following project, of a willow stag with a hedgerow frame, is a three-day workshop that I host, in which we begin by sourcing and processing our hedgerow frame, with a focus on respecting habitat and on consideration for plants and the creatures that live there.

Many animals can be constructed using this method. The advantage of utilising a hedgerow frame is that the materials are local, cost-effective, biodegradable, and supportive of a traditional way of land management. When making wooden-framed sculptures as commissions, I keep the whole construction completely natural, with simple, round wood mortise-and-tenon joints, which I peg with willow (see Chapter 4).

"Sheep on Holway Hill" (c. 2008). Made with Somerset steamed and white willow over a hedgerow hazel frame.

The stag demonstrated in this chapter is being made by super-student, Lindsay. During the three-day willow-weaving workshop we used screws and annular ring shank nails, due to time constraints.

Equipment and tools required

- Notebook, pencil, ruler, and reference pictures, for working out design, frame, and measurements;
- covering paper, and chalk, for transposing and enlarging your design on a wall;
- bow saw / pruning saw / hand saw, for harvesting wood, cutting to size, and trimming;
- billhook, for snedding and splitting;
- bit and brace / drill and craft knife, for simple mortise-and-tenon joints, or annular ring shank nails, hammer, and drill bit slightly thinner than the nails, for pilot holes;
- secateurs, for trimming the willow;
- kettle, matches, and cup – for essential cups of tea.

Materials required

- Round wooden poles for the frame;
- 50 willow withies 210 cm (7 feet) in length and a variety of smaller sizes for the main body;
- white willow for detail.

Making the frame

🌿 **Step 1.** Draw the side profile of your sculpture, ensuring that it is proportionally correct, and then draw the frame within. It is important that the frame will not interfere with the external lines of the sculpture when complete, so do allow a good few inches of room for the willow to be laid on top. The frame is basically a four-legged table, and the more it is like a table frame, the less likely will the sculpture be to topple.

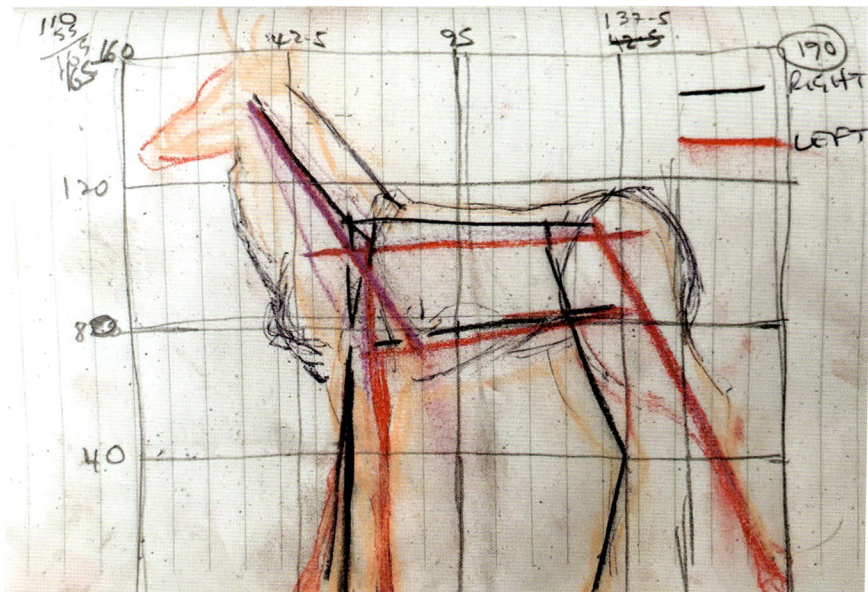

I would suggest that at least three of the legs should be pretty straight for stability. You will see in this image that we have then added neck bracing for supporting the head and antlers. The more structure the frame provides, the less structural willow you will have to use. When happy with the drawing, create a grid over the top – this will facilitate the transposition from small idea to large sculpture, as you will be able to work out your proportions accordingly. In this case, the grid is divided to make 16 squares of equal size. Mark the grid with the measurements that you would like your sculpture to achieve.

Step 2. Transpose your design onto a wall, so you have a life-size image to help you with construction. These days I like to use a large piece of paper, as I have run out of wall space and this method allows me to keep records of all of the frames that I have made.

Draw a grid that represents the finished size, dividing it into the same number of squares that you have on your initial drawing. This allows you to draw the shape of your sculpture using the proportions in your drawing, as you can easily compare which parts of the shape fit into which squares. Add the lines of the frame to the image, and you can easily measure the length of the pieces of hazel required for the framework. For a simple sculpture such as this, I have found a side profile to be adequate.

Step 3.
Cut your rods to size. Think about how the sculpture will be standing: you may like to cut the leg sticks longer, so you have length enough to insert them into the ground if the sculpture is to stand on earth, or into a plinth, for stability, or you may wish to cut them at the feet if the sculpture is to be free-standing. Keep your offcuts, as they may well come in handy for joining and supporting the two side frames.

If you have any pieces of wood that are not straight, think about how you can incorporate them into the frame to enhance the shape. Lindsay is using a bent piece of hazel to accentuate the hock of the deer.

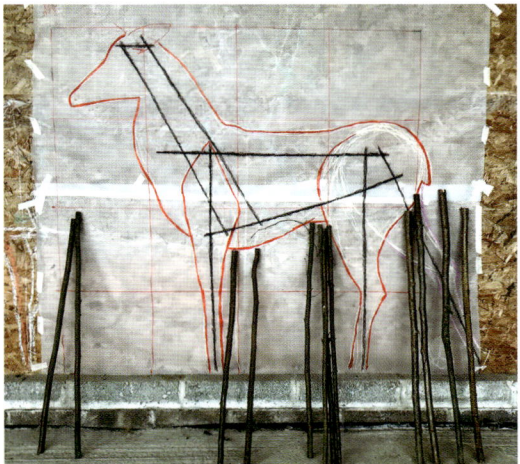

❋ **Step 4.**   Make one side of the frame at a time, using your choice of joints (see Chapter 4). The two sides will be constructed as mirror images, to ensure that the legs are on the outside of the frame on each side. When the two side frames are made, they will need some bracing diagonals to prevent movement. Add these with a jointing method of your choice. If you are using nails for these diagonals, you will probably be able to use hazel off-cuts; you may find attaching easier if you cut the round wood to size and then cleave it into two, carefully using your billhook. Join the two sides together, again using cleft hazel or round wood, ensuring that the feet are far enough apart to offer stability without the frame being so wide that it interferes with the finished outside shape of the sculpture. If you are using nails or screws, be very careful not to have tips sticking through the wood, as they may cause you injury as you weave. Whenever using nails or screws, it is helpful to drill a pilot hole first, in order to prevent the wood splitting along the grain. In green wood the pilot hole should be marginally smaller than the width of the nail or screw, as the hole will become wider as the wood seasons. Be particularly aware of the location of the top corners of the frame, as they have a tendency to stick up too far and interfere with the soft, flowing lines of the shoulders and the rump. When you have a good solid "table frame", add the required appendages: in this case, the neck support.

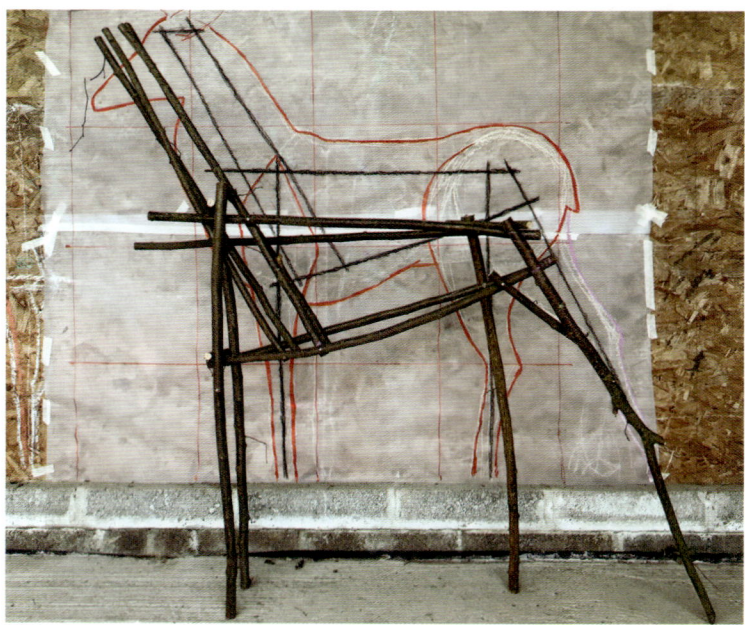

Creating the shape

🌿 **Step 5.** Now that your basic internal frame is constructed and supported with diagonals, it is time to begin introducing the wicker work.

Consistent with the GRT, begin with your thicker weavers. Consider the curves created by using the "back" or "belly" of the withy: gradually build up the main body shape, using the framework to tuck the butt ends of the willow behind and the tension caused by opposing pressure to gain curves. Add around the chest cavity from front to back and back to front, and then around the chest cavity from side to side. Remember that the sculpture will only get bigger,

so take care not to reach the final size quite yet: this part is all about creating a basic proportional shape; the finishing detail will come later. Be mindful of the curves caused by the musculoskeletal system of the animal and build the sculpture up accordingly, so these natural curves are not lost. Begin with the central core – the thoracic and abdominal areas – then add, separately, each leg and the neck. Keep referring to reference pictures. As with all of the sculptures, create a shape with thicker withies, and then reinforce that shape with finer ones. Work your way around the sculpture, building it up evenly so as not to put too much emphasis on any one part. You are aiming for an even latticework all over the body, so wherever you see a big gap, dissect it with a weaver. Work with the flow of the willow, which has a force of its own and will let you know where it wants to go and where it doesn't. Ensure you are taking your sticks in all directions and that you are weaving them into the existing body, for strength and density, rather than just going round and round on top, in which case you will lose your shape and have a baggy finish with little defined shape. Use the butt end of a withy to weave in and out of the existing body (like a needle sewing through material) for about half of the sticks' length, which should anchor the thick end of your osier and allow you to then easily weave away the tip end.

You require enough coverage to create a good foundation, but not enough to inhibit weaving in the finishing detail.

Be prepared to stop looking at your work for a while. It may be a good idea to walk away and return with a fresh eye. Sometimes it helps to take a picture and look at that, which seems, strangely, to allow one to be more objective.

Step 6. When you are happy with the strength and proportions of your stag, it is time to add the head. I have found that making the "skull" of the head separately and then introducing it to the body allows for more character and movement. A word of warning: a common error at this point is to make the head too big, so err on the side of daintiness!

Following the GRT, begin by making the shape and then reinforcing it, from side to side, with finer weavers. Remember that, when adding willow in order to position and reinforce the head, it will grow in size. If you get the opportunity to examine an actual skull of the animal that you are creating, then please have a close look at nature's brilliant construction. This level of insight will assist your

accurate portrayal immensely. Place the stag's willow skull on the top of the neck, then take some time fine-tuning the height and position, ensuring that the turn of the head is compliant with the posture of the body of the sculpture. When you are satisfied, use finer weavers to attach the head to the neck.

Step 7.

By now the body is formed and in proportion, the head is on and creating character, but the legs are looking on the skinny side, so it's time to work on those.

The hazel frame is providing the rigidity, the willow will provide shape. Keep looking at your reference pictures and you will see that from the knee down the leg of the deer is really just bone and tendons, so avoid building the bottom half of the leg up too much. You require

withies that reach to the foot and still have the tip length to weave through the body. The exact number of sticks will vary according to the thickness of the willow you are using and the size of the sculpture. You are aiming to pass the butt end of the withy in a downward direction, through diverse parts of the body of the sculpture, to the tips of the toes. Ideally, the distribution of the leg sticks will also bulk out the upper portion of the leg, where the muscle is.

When you have threaded your leg sticks down, hold them together with a temporary fixing (baler twine shown here) while you fix them tidily with a willow wrap (see Chapter 4). You may like to position the wraps to represent the prominent knee and ankle joints of the animal.

Adding the detail

✿ **Step 8.** At this point you should be seeing a proportional shape with an even coverage of willow but little detail, which we will begin to add now. Return to the head of your creature and begin the antlers.

For this creation we will be using willow for the antlers. You may, of course, like to use other materials for antlers, such as aptly shaped branches of trees (I have found the growth patterns of elm to be particularly representative of the tines of a stag's antlers), or even real antlers, although I would point out that the light-weight hazel frame that we have constructed this sculpture upon may not be suitable for anything heavier than willow antlers. For heavier antlers you would probably want to construct a stronger internal head and neck frame in order to support the weight of them. I would generally use a metal frame for such support (see Chapter 8, "Metal Frames").

✢ **Step 9.** It is fairly straightforward to construct well-attached antlers with willow. Begin by inserting the butt end of a medium-thickness weaver into each side of the head, where the antlers would grow; push far enough so you have the tip of each stick proud on one side while still having its butt end prominent on the other, so you have two withies that are not going to fall off sticking out of each side of the head. Use finer weavers to hold them in the desired location at the skull. Bend the tip ends of the antlers back on themselves, and spiral down the length of the antlers. Take some white willow; insert the butt ends into the skull and then wrap up and down the antlers (see chapter 4). If you require more antler tines, then extend the white willow out in the direction required, then bend back on itself, to create a pointy tine, and wrap around that structure.

✣ **Step 10.** When the antlers are complete, position the ears. Do bear in mind that animals' ears are hugely expressive, so take your time to ensure that the position of the ears in consistent with the posture of your animal. (Use the method described for ears in Chapter 4).

❀ Step 11. Your sculpture is now completely covered with a random weave and is ready for detailed finishing with your finest willow. You may choose to use multiple strands (see Chapter 4). Think about weaving in the direction that will indicate the features you want to present: you could direct the willow to be consistent with the hair grain, but as deer are so lean, muscle tissue is a defining factor of their appearance, so you may wish to concentrate on that. Work evenly around the sculpture, getting those essential movement lines in place. While you are adding the finish, ensure that the shape that you have worked so hard to refine does not get lost but, instead, becomes denser and more organised. You can preserve the gentle undulations by working on the anatomy from the central core outward – for example, the back, belly, chest, and neck first, followed by each of the legs muscles.

How dense you make your final weave will be down to stylistic and practical considerations. As you add willow, your gaps get smaller, and you will need finer willow. Sometimes my sculptures get so intricate I've had to use rug and crochet hooks to extract withy tips from tiny holes.

"Doe" (2018) and "Stag" (2022). [Made by Lindsay Higgins]

8

Metal frames

Metal frames do, definitely, have their advantages. They don't rot and therefore hold their shape for longer than a wooden frame; as a result the willow coverage lasts longer, as it is decoration rather than structure. Metal frames can have foot plates welded at the base, allowing them to be easily secured to the ground, which may be essential in public places.

The added strength of the structure facilitates easier transportation, even as the sculpture ages. Any willow parts that get damaged are easily reparable without having to rebuild the sculpture from scratch.

The malleable properties of metal allow shapes to be made that would be nigh-on impossible with willow alone. Twists and turns are made easy, delicate appendages made strong. Top-heavy, overextended forms can be created with very little ground contact area required at the base.

Sounds great! But to be honest, I'd rather make with natural materials . . . which I'm sure is no surprise to you, the reader, by this point in the book.

The whole process and energy requirements of willow sculpture change drastically the moment a metal frame is incorporated. Reliance on outside sources leads the associated carbon footprint to shoot up, as the metal rods come from an energy-hungry industry. Add to

◄ *"Ballerina" (c. 2020). The metal frame, welded to a pegged-down plate, allows the balanced and gracefully extended dancer to stand on point.*

that the increased transportation and the welding . . . in the grand scheme of things it may be a drop in the ocean, but even so, all of these little things add up – and is it really necessary? These are the issues I grapple with.

Due to these considerations, I am not a huge fan of metal frames. That's not to say they can't be beautiful and serve a valid purpose, but I do wonder when a willow sculpture stops being a willow sculpture and starts being a metal sculpture with willow on it. This concept gets muddy to me when it is the metal providing the structural shape, rather than the willow. Metal frames are great if you want to do less with the willow. My style of metal frame is minimalistic. You will find your own way.

Planning the metal frame

Begin by doodling a couple of sketches of how you imagine your sculpture to look, from different angles. Play with some different postures. If you don't fancy drawing, then find some reference pictures and print them out, so you can draw notes and measurements on them. When you are happy with your design, scale it up proportionally: draw a grid over the picture and then a full-sized grid of the same proportions on a large piece of paper, a wall, the floor, or whatever else is to hand. By matching the contents of the grids one square at a time, you will build up a full-sized, proportional representation of your drawing, which you will be able to use as a template for your metal work.

"Ballerina" (c. 2020).   *The side and rear view were transposed from pad to wall: a grid was drawn over the picture and scaled up.*

"Ballerina" (c. 2020). The picture from the wall was traced onto paper, to be used as a template for shaping the metal frame.

Making the metal frame

Personally, I do not like working with metal. I don't like the noise, the smell, or the energy. Metal is so cold and dead in the hands, it needs so much fire to revive it. Nothing like weaving with willow. I choose to take my designs to people who do enjoy it. When I began to work with metal fabricators, I used to make it up as we went along. I would draw shapes on the floor with chalk, which the blacksmith would match with bent rods. It was fun but not very time-efficient. I have sped up the process by creating full-sized patterns of the metal shapes required in advance. The metal is bent to shape and then the sculpture is welded together, one piece at a time, assessing the exact position of each part as it is assembled. Attention to detail is critical, as the frame will strongly influence the form and feeling of the outcome.

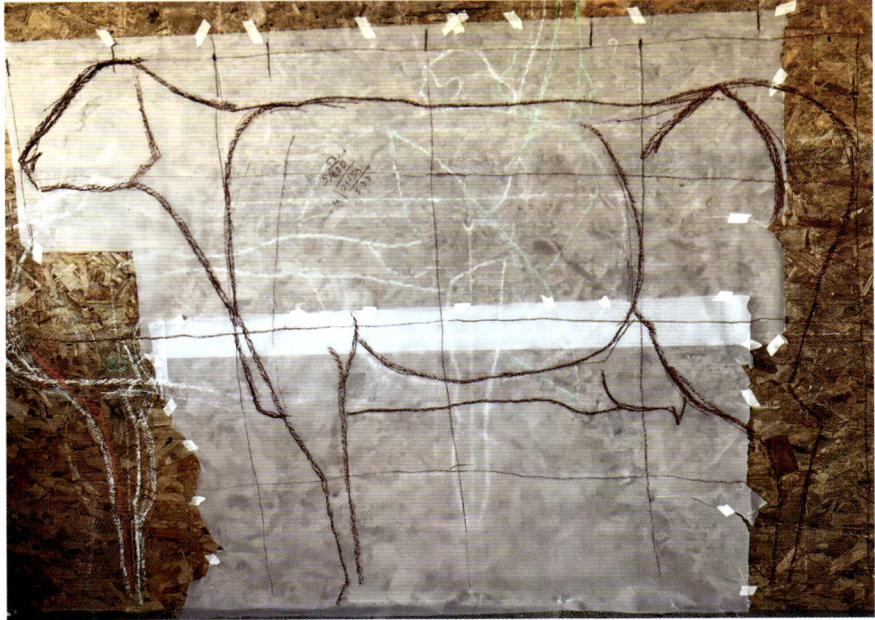

"Holstein" (c. 2023). Drawn straight on paper, instead of drawing on the wall. A side-view reference picture was used, which had a grid drawn over it, allowing straightforward proportional transfer to full size of the internal frame design.

◀ **"Holstein"** (c. 2023). *The metalworker, Matt, was able to use the full-size design as a template to shape the metal rods.*

"Holstein" (c. 2023). *Side profile pieces are made to fit the pattern.*

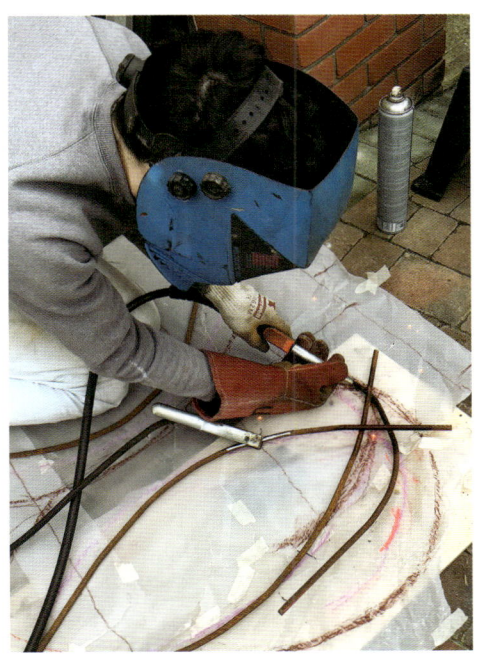

➤ *"Holstein" (c. 2023).* Matt joins the two sides together first, before standing them up and adding cross pieces for a three-dimensional form.

"Holstein" (c.2023). Frame finished, primed, and internal support for the willow added.

Foot plates are attached for secure fixing. The foot plates may have been pre-drilled with peg holes.

Metal frames do offer the advantage of being able to hold metal plates on which to bolt heavy things . . . such as antlers. Needless to say, I do not take the use of real antlers lightly.

The frame is painted with primer, to prevent rust runs. Following that I use (recycled) chicken wire to create a shell around the frame. The wire mesh is completely covered with willow and provides internal support for the weaving. This added reinforcement increases longevity of the sculpture. My style of framework is very light on metal; I elect to use as little as possible.

When the frame is built, primed, and the internal reinforcement is in place, the weaving can begin. The GRT applies, starting with thicker willow and decreasing the size as the sculpture progresses. As the structure is ready-made, you will begin with fairly fine weavers. The "skeleton" is in place, so you will be looking at the muscular structure. Metal frames allow a style of weaving that is particularly fine and regimented when used for non-growing willow sculptures, but can also be used to support living willow sculptures, providing a static frame that the plant can be trained around.

"Holstein" (c.2023). *Ready for transportation to new home.*

"Stag" (c. 2014). Two sides, joined together, just as with the willow stag with a hedgerow frame (Chapter 7). Note the holes in the foot plates for pegs. The metalwork has been primed with red oxide to prevent rust.

"Stag" (c. 2014).

"Living Elephants" (c. 2009). *Living willow sculptures with internal metal frames.*

"Living Elephants" (c. 2015). Elephant and calf are left to grow free all year and are given some TLC once annually. Despite the infrequent weaving, the metal frame offers a consistent shape.

Preserving the sculpture

The metalwork will provide support and be long-lasting, but for best results the willow should be treated. I do not use chemical sprays, I choose to use natural plant-based oil and wax preparations. When the sculpture is finished and completely dry, I apply two coats of a nourishing, waterproof UV-protection oil. I recommend that each year the sculpture, when dry, is dusted off with a stiff brush and another coat of protective oil applied. If the sculpture is to be kept outside all year round, then you may want to repeat the application more often. The point of the treatment is to provide a rain jacket. Without a coat of oil, the dry willow will become brittle within a few years, dependent on exposure.

Willow will rot, thank goodness, but we would like to slow it down a bit sometimes.

If your sculpture is made of buff or white stripped willow, then it will weather, turning silvery and then mottled and dull, before falling apart. Ensuring effective oil treatment will slow this process. Sometimes the weathering process will be undesirable. Preparations can be bought to "re-whiten" weathered wood; I've not tried them, so I can't comment. Another option is to paint the sculpture, and this I have done, with good effect.

"Roger's Bull" (c. 2016). A metal frame and wire reinforcement facilitates extremely fine weaving, while also protecting the fellow from being trampled by an escaped herd of extremely interested lady cows (true!).

"Roger's Bull" (c. 2016). The three-strand technique in pliable white willow allows detail and movement, with the lines of the willow creating a dynamic energy through the muscle structure. The weave is tight and dense. The internal metal is invisible.

"Roger's Bull" (2023). Although this sculpture has been standing outside in an exposed location, with very little preservative treatment and the occasional amorous encounter with escapee cows, for 7 years, the metal frame and internal wire reinforcement ensures that the sculpture is still in good order. The white willow has weathered a silvery grey.

"Rob" (c. 2020).   Frame built, primed, reinforced, and ready for weaving.

METAL FRAMES

"Rob" (c. 2020). The subdued golden willow, dried and soaked for use, lends itself perfectly to the red deer stag, pictured in front of a clump of coppiced willow.

"Reindeer" (c. 2019). The frames offer secure fixing and the strength to withstand frequent changes of location. The metal rod allows the antlers to be full-sized, slender, strong. Each of the antlers' metal tines has been looped over to reduce risk of injury.

"Leaping Hare" (c. 2021). Metal frames allow top-heavy and unbalanced sculpture to stand, creating leaping effects.

Photo by David and Carol Marks

9

Weaving a living willow sculpture

What deep, soulful joy it is to commune with a living being, to play, to laugh, to cry, to create. We so often take our slow, steady plant brethren for granted as we rush from A to B, like ants on amphetamine. Time takes on a different meaning when your hands are on the bark of a branch, gently twisting and tweaking with care and compassion as you work together to create extra meaning or resonance within your

space of being. Spending time working with willow moves emotional energetics through your psyche as you become absorbed . . . the more you get into it, the more you get out of it.

◄ *"Howling Wolves" (c. 2004).*

There's magic in them there branches! Tune in to the feel of a live stick and compare with a dead one. Feel the intangible background buzz of life's energy. Meet with the dynamic, vibrant willow wand, and you'll start noticing nature's silent noise everywhere.

As sap starts to rise in spring, hold the tips of the growing twigs as you would a child's hand. Feel the zing from the wakening earth rise to your palms, along your arms, into your very core, down your legs and back into the ground through your rooted feet. This is you being part of Earth's energetic cycle . . . ah, we are blessed indeed. . . .

As Earth's hyperactive humans, we seem to have a mission to manipulate our environment, but not always the wisdom to temper that desire. Living willow sculpture is about re-establishing our connection with our own evolution, embracing and celebrating the woven web that holds together us humans, other animals, plants, and fungi, with our living planet.

Each sculpture, even if made the same way and placed just a few metres from another, will face differing environmental variabilities, ensuring they develop in their own way. It is these unique developments that make living willow sculpture so exciting and dynamic.

"Golden Unicorn" (c. 2000). One of the original living unicorns, with no internal frame, the natural bark colour creating the stunning effect.

"Golden Unicorn" (c. 2002). *The living pieces remain golden, but the original weavers have dried and faded. Growth is widely present, with concentrated areas directly above the ground points and benefitting from full sun.*

Locating a living willow sculpture

You may have a location in mind for your willow sculpture, and you may have to work with what you've got, but there are points to consider that will affect the growing plant. It would be wise to consider these before you decide where to place your living sculpture.

Soil

Living willow sculptures will thrive in some areas and struggle in others, but there will be certain varieties of willow that are suited to particular soil types. It would be worth taking a look at the soil in your area and any varieties of willow that appear to be thriving there. The subject of soil is huge: you will no doubt find a weighty tome to impart all the particulars. For the purposes of this book, I want to avoid falling down that earthy rabbit hole and, instead, just keep it simple: if you can grow good grass (I don't mean the recreational variety), you can grow a happy willow sculpture (as long as you keep the grass under control while the willow is becoming established).

Drainage

Willow is associated with water and does prefer wet locations, but it does not like to stand in soggy wellies. Stagnant or brackish water is not ideal for willow sculptures. Although some varieties may tolerate swampy conditions and have an important ecological role in such places, willows will prefer a well-drained but damp, nutrient-rich site, which is why they seem to do so well along the bank of a river or stream, with the constant movement of groundwater filtering through the roots, towards the water course. The growth of withies is noticeably improved by an adequate water supply throughout the growing season.

Rooting

When constructing your living willow sculpture, you will most likely be planting cuttings, which will, if conditions are favourable, develop rootlets from their leaf nodes underground. Bearing in mind that you are not planting short cuttings, but long cuttings that will be woven into the sculpture, you are asking a lot from willow's wonder-rooting ability. Let's ensure that we give the dear little stick the best chance to grow into a healthy tree. If the ground is very stoney, a lack of nutrient-rich organic matter and water to feed the developing roots may be a problem. For the first few years, new roots are vulnerable to extremes, particularly drought and weed competition. Your attention to these details will greatly affect the plant's ability to thrive. The cutting will have to be inserted into the ground deep enough for it to take root and remain stable, with access to the earth's water-retaining capacity. This will vary from site to site. On favourable soil I would want the cuttings to be at least 30 cm (one foot) in the ground, and probably deeper on well-drained soil. Watering during prolonged dry spells may be essential during the first two or three summers. A heavy soaking every few days is better than a little bit daily. It's fine to use your bath water: the willow outside my bath shed seems to love it.

Weeds

As previously mentioned, for the first few years the plant will be vulnerable to being outcompeted by weeds – particularly perennials such as docks, nettles, brambles, and couch grass. I certainly would not want to eradicate these plants, which have their own thing going on, are essential for wildlife, and are some of my favoured herbal allies. But until the willow is established, the enthusiasm of such perennials may be a little overbearing for the tender, young willow. It is advisable to prepare the ground by removing the roots of perennials (please use a spade, not poison). When the plant is established, it will provide its own weed suppressant mulch in the form of discarded leaves, but until that point it will need a bit of help. I favour biodegradable mulches, such as wood chips, cardboard, or sheep's wool, or just content myself with hand weeding around the plant for a few years. I do not like to use plastic-based mulching sheets of any type, as they break down into micro-plastics. Once you've put them there, you'll never get rid of them. Don't be tempted to plant through a thick plastic weed-control membrane, as it may well prevent vital flow of nutrients as the trunks of the sculpture widen. For the same reason ensure that there is no plastic or metal topsoil reinforcement, which would inhibit the growth of the sculpture's living uprights.

Weather

Prevailing wind direction and exposure should be considered when determining the position of your sculpture. The stronger the wind, the firmer the sculpture needs to be. If the sculpture is to be in a particularly exposed area, then you may like to ensure the design is an aerodynamic shape. If your sculpture is constantly battered by a side-on gale, then it may well lean, or even topple. Exposure to light must also be considered: the amount of sun the sculpture receives will make a huge difference to the success of the plant. When maintaining an established willow sculpture, the growth is always a strong indicator of which side is North (little growth), and which side is South (loads of growth). If the sculpture is to be sited under trees, then it may be better to have a non-living willow sculpture, as living willow is not a fan of shady conditions.

Obstacles

Consider what obstacles will be affecting the sculpture as it grows, above ground and below. Every part of the sculpture must be accessible for weaving, trimming, and maintenance. During maintenance, a ladder may be necessary, in which case the ground must be level enough to safely stand one. There may be existing infrastructure, such as fencing, which will inhibit movement around the sculpture. Obstacles may block the view of the finished sculpture, or create too much shade. Remember to consider underground infrastructure that may be affected by the root system – such as water pipes or building foundations. Extensive rooting can be an advantage at times – for example, when reducing soil erosion or aiding filtration – but your neighbours might not be happy if the powerful root system of an established willow sculpture begins to burrow its way into their cellar.

* * *

These pre-planting considerations are variabilities that will influence the development of the sculpture after it has been created and set free to grow into its own personality. Just as with the rest of us, the unique set of challenges and benefits that the plant sculpture encounters from conception until death will shape its life-long development. Gentle, guiding support from you will ensure that the sculpture grows to be strong in its own character.

Just as in nature, a frame is required to provide structure and strength.

Sometimes the frame will be more of an exoskeleton: an external skeleton that supports and protects an animal's body. In nature this is most commonly seen in insect-like or sea creatures. Think of the outer surface of a crab, for example, or a woodlouse: both rely on their exoskeleton for structure and strength. Willow sculptures that are bottom-heavy and have a continuous base line in connection with the earth will likely not require an independent internal frame.

In common with our mammal brethren and wider family of reptiles, birds, fish, and amphibians, we have endoskeletons that provide structure and strength and are crucial for movement. Certain shapes of living willow sculptures benefit enormously from an internal frame. When creating quadrupeds with a top-heavy shape and small grounding points, I incorporate an internal frame. Originally I did not include independent frames, but watching the development of living willow sculptures over decades has shown the importance of internal support and particularly how invaluable it is during the "awkward teenage years".

When the sculpture is first created, it will be strong, as all of the non-living willow used in construction will be intact. After two or three years much of the original non-living willow will have started to become brittle, but the living willow will not yet be able to offer strength to the shape. Depending on the size of the sculpture and the variety of willow, the living part of the sculpture may take a further two or three years to achieve coverage required for integrity. This in-between stage is what I refer to as the "awkward teenage years": the time in its life when the sculpture is most difficult, requiring the most patience and tender loving care. With gentle guidance and support, the sculpture will pass this point, and

◀ **"Living Willow Hare"** (c. 2003). Entering its first summer, approximately 3 metres (10 feet) tall, made only with bio-fuel willow, gathered from the site. Due to the upright shape, no internal frame was required. All willow growth will be gently guided through the outer layer of weaving, aiming for even distribution.

▶ **"Living Willow Hare"** (c. 2006). The growth coverage is healthy, but strategic weaving will be required at the base of the sculpture. The hare-plant tower is home to myriad insects; bitter vetch climbs, providing an adornment of purple blooms. A bird nests inside the chest.

➤ *"Living Willow Hare" (c. 2015). In winter the sculpture is apparent and developed in character. No longer lithe and light, the hare-plant has become substantial. Most new growth will be removed, with any weaker points reinforced with withies growing lower down.*

◄ *"Living Willow Hare" (c. 2016). The hare moves through its second decade with an impressive cloak of green slung over one shoulder, towards the sun. Some of the original uprights are now trunks, providing a firm core to the sculpture. As the plant is now established, it can withstand some light summer pruning (see "Maintaining a Living Willow Sculpture"), so the shape can be enjoyed throughout the year.*

you can pride yourself on a job most wonderfully done while you watch the maturing feature flourish!

I have considered treating the non-living part of the sculpture, in the hope I could extend its supportive capabilities. However, the manner of treatment would probably involve biocidal chemicals, which would be completely inappropriate on a sculpture designed to celebrate and enhance life. Alternatively some type of oil could be applied, but that may interfere with insect life or encourage animals to eat the sculpture.

Further to the practical considerations is the desire to create a sculpture that works with natural cycles . . . the life–death–rot–rebirth cycle being one of these: the sculpture rots, providing habitat and nutrients for life; the sculpture grows, providing habitat and nutrients for life. I choose to embrace and work with this cycle of life, rather than engaging in a futile fight against it.

"Howling Wolves" (c. 2003). Coppiced ash and willow were gathered from the site and a simple frame constructed.

"Howling Wolves" (c. 2003). When built, the giant lupines were imposing figures in the open landscape.

"Howling Wolves" (c. 2006). Growth is good, and original weaving remains. This living willow sculpture is about to enter its tricky stage. The weaving has weakened, and new growth is not yet robust. During the next few years it will be vital to ensure new growth is used to unite and strengthen the shape.

Photo by Ronnie Cresswell

"Howling Wolves" (c. 2015). One of the pair holds its upright, howling shape and is strong throughout. Living weaving can be seen, green and growing evenly around the sculpture.

"Howling Wolves" (c. 2016). Every moment of every day, year in, year out, the sculpture changes, grows, and supports intricate webs of wonder.

***"Howling Wolves"* (c. 2015).**   *The partner wolf has developed differently, now crouching, growling, and snarling. During the "awkward teenage years" new growth was trimmed, rather than being encouraged into the shell. This resulted in division as the top-heavy head of the sculpture, separating from the back end, fell forward. The remedy was to let the plant grow unhindered for one full annual cycle and the following winter to use the abundant growth to influence and reinforce the position that the wolf-plant had chosen to take. Rest and restore!*

"Howling Wolves" (c. 2016). From "Howling Wolf" to "Growling Wolf", this sculpture beautifully demonstrates life being uniquely shaped by external pressures beyond its control.

With living willow sculptures, I prefer to use natural materials that have been sourced from the location where the sculpture is to live. The purpose of the frame is to provide strength, particularly while the plant is becoming self-standing. It must be placed in the earth at a depth that will retain security, even when the sculpture is being battered by a force-9 gale, its leaves acting as a sail. Consider size, weather exposure, shape of sculpture, and soil type, as all influence depth of frame.

> *Warning: Avoid sculpture strangulation. Although a piece of baling twine, cable tie, or a wire twist may be helpful during the build, it is crucial that such items are not left in place.*
>
> *The centre of a willow stem is structurally supportive, while the willow's essential nutrients are transported under the surface of the bark. As the Salix stem thickens, immoveable restrictions cut off vital flow and slowly garrotte the plant to death. For this reason, it is essential that only willow ties are used on living willow sculptures.*

Creating a sculpture with materials gathered from the area in which the sculpture will be situated is so engaging and absorbing. I find the greatest satisfaction in having made a beautiful spirit-thing when working that closely with nature. It takes time and adaptability, for sure, but the process offers you a connection to the land and your own skill development that you would not otherwise experience. A sculpture created in such a way will have an authenticity, being something of the landscape, rather than something plonked upon it. Local would have been the norm just a few generations ago, yet the concept has grown so alien to us in our days of shadow acres. Living willow sculpture can be truly of the land where you stand, a celebration of place and time.

It may not always be possible to create a sculpture utilising only materials that have grown close to hand, but I would still favour materials indigenous to the area, which biodegrade. The sculpture will contribute to the life–death–reabsorption life cycle, without contributing to the plethora of pervading pollutants that we are littering over our land.

Additional manufactured fixings (such as wire, screws, cable ties, etc.) are unnecessary. We humans have been gifted with ingenuity, and nature provides us with materials. With just a little effort we can reclaim the skills we've exchanged for something bought in plastic packaging.

When working with found materials, it is problematic to become too prescriptive about the exact type and size of materials that you will need. Part of the process is to absorb oneself in an area and be adaptable with what is available. Resourcefulness of such environmental intimacy may seem difficult at first but, with time and patience, mists rise and actions become clear.

"Shire Horse and Seeker" (c. 2009). *Frame materials for the 19-hand-high shire horse were gathered nearby. The curvy pieces of found wood accentuated shapes representative of the animal. Freshly cut, coloured varieties of willow were brought from my withy bed. When the shell was begun, living willow uprights were dispersed through the body, butt ends plunging down the legs and into the ground.*

***"Shire Horse and Seeker"* (c. 2009).** *Sculpture taken from a legend of a knight wh seeks far and wide for his lost love. Eventually, he wearily stumbles into a glade, wher he sees her dancing with the Faerie folk. As he watches her, enchanted, he becomes roote and cannot move.*

The type of willow that you choose for your sculpture will influence the growth. Due to a fondness for hybridisation, there are literally hundreds of varieties of willow. Among those varieties, there will be further differences, due to diverse soil and climatic conditions. During the making process the name we give the willow is unimportant. What matters is what can be done with the withies. When working with willow for a while, one begins to recognise each stick and what it will do. With a gradual fine-tuning of senses, the process becomes intuitive.

Willows growing in an area will show you if they are happy, and may even provide cuttings for your sculpture. Otherwise, look at your soil and select a variety that suits the site and your practical requirements. Varieties that offer vigorous growth may be excellent for large sculptures but completely unmanageable for smaller pieces. Bark colour may also be a factor in choosing, with all or part of the sculpture being made with brightly coloured willow to enhance features.

A combination of varieties may be used to add texture and interest to the form, such as the twisted growth of a *tortuosa* variety or the weeping growth of a *Salix babylonica*. Keep in mind, though, that the reason willow works for living sculptures is because it consistently grows long straight shoots that can be woven into the structure to provide a strong shell – an even lattice of living willow. The contorted and weeping varieties will not offer the same properties and may not be appropriate for the main structural work.

Photo by Chris Groves

"Shire Horse and Seeker" (c. 2009). *The rooted knight and his horse turn into a tree, where he helplessly stands longing for his lost love. Just two months after completion, the sculpture shows visible growth as the plant begins its journey through life, at the whim of a thousand variables.*

Willow plants do have basic growth patterns according to type, with some growing stout and thick, others tall and slender. When constructing a living willow sculpture, there will be main uprights that grow, but also non-growing, middling sizes for structure and support, and finer withies for the weaves and ties. The GRT applies: begin with thick osiers and progressively use finer withies as the sculpture progresses.

You may like to have a stroll around the area looking at established willow trees. If there are apparent plant pathogens that appear troublesome, choose resistant varieties. Having said that, I have been growing willow for well over 20 years, without the use of any chemical biocides, and have always found willow to be resilient if it has enough water, sunshine, and weed control and doesn't have its new shoots nibbled away by browsers in the spring.

Willow cuttings for sculptures must be taken when the plant is dormant during the winter months. Traditionally, in the UK, cutting time is between November and March. The time to cut is after the autumnal leaf drop and before the leaf buds appear in spring.

Cut and bundle the willow you require, as described in "Harvesting the Withy Bed" in Chapter 3, and use for the sculpture fairly soon. It certainly wouldn't do any harm to leave the freshly cut willow rods for a couple of weeks. How long they remain viable for rooting will depend on how quickly they dry out. Most freshly cut withies remain viable until the start of spring if kept under a hedge (in shady, damp conditions), but this is completely weather-dependent. If you are concerned that conditions are dry, or you are heading into spring, then stand the bolt, butts down, in a bucket of water. If left in water, the rods will begin to develop rootlets from the submerged nodes, and leaves will appear on the stem. These can still be used for living willow sculpture when the sap is rising but will have the disadvantage of being less flexible and having vulnerable rootlets that may be damaged during insertion into the ground.

If you are using willow plants that already have an established root ball, you can plant them at any time of year. The stems will be less forgiving upon bending when sap is in the plant, so they will have to be incorporated into the shape very carefully. Ensure heavy watering of the root ball *in situ* for the first couple of years.

The process of constructing a living willow sculpture is fairly straightforward: design, make the frame, insert the living uprights, and reinforce – that's it, in a nutshell. Let me guide you through that process in more detail.

Equipment and tools required

- Notebook, pencil, ruler, and reference pictures, for working out the design, frame, and measurements;
- bow saw / pruning saw, for harvesting wood, cutting to size, and trimming;
- billhook, for snedding and splitting;
- bit and brace / drill and craft knife; for simple mortice-and-tenon joints;
- spade, for positioning the frame deep into the ground;
- heavy-duty spike (I use my horse's old tether spike) and lump hammer, for making holes in the ground into which to insert the living willow rods;
- secateurs, for trimming the willow;
- kettle, matches, and cup, for essential cups of tea (I like to infuse herbs I find on site).

As we are using only natural materials found close by, tools will help. You may be surprised that I'm not going to recommend knapping a piece of flint, although, of course, you could. I have a great scar on my hand as a reminder of a basketry demonstration at a reconstructed Neolithic settlement and the keen edge of a little stone blade.

Planning the living willow sculpture

Using your pad and pencil, draw the side profile of your finished sculpture. Think about its relationship to the ground: is it standing on four legs or not? Consider whether the shape is balanced or off-balance, and what kind of support will be required to prevent the sculpture toppling over.

If the frame is to be an "exoskeleton" rather than an "endoskeleton", then the living willow should be planted so it grows in a straight upwards line for the greatest chance of success. Angles of 45° from the vertical are acceptable. Unhindered flow is imperative in the long cuttings while root stock is under-developed.

If opting for an internal frame, draw the shape of the frame to fit inside the picture that you have drawn. Ensure that the frame is supportive without affecting the eventual outer layer of the sculpture. The frame itself will probably be completely hidden: it should offer strength without interfering with the external lines of the willow. Be mindful of corners on box sections of the frame, as, if they stand proud, they can interfere with the smooth shape of the sculpture. When designing the frame, you may find that using triangles with ridgepoles, rather than squares, will lead to a smoother shape. You may be fortunate and find unusual, twisted wood to work with and use to create certain shapes. Don't be tempted to over-complicate the frame: work with the shape of the wood you have, and keep it simple.

Vulnerable appendages should be supported, either with the frame or by direct line of growth from the willow. If you have horizontal appendages, then construct a basic frame first and then affix the extra pieces. The additions will be more secure if they are fixed at two or more points.

Consider the depth an internal frame should be inserted into the ground: the type of soil and wind exposure will make a difference, as will the shape of the sculpture. If the sculpture is top-heavy or off balance, then more depth will be required to stabilise the frame.

It may take some time to work out the skeleton, but it is time well spent, as the framework will guide the rest of the sculpture process, allowing an easier build and more straightforward maintenance.

Transfer design to materials

Take your sketch and draw a grid over it, with representation of the finished dimensions, as this will allow to you to work out the measurements of the frame wood you will need. We are working from a two-dimensional side profile, so there will be a slight discrepancy in measurements, as there is no account of foreshortening, but hey ho, it's not rocket science. When cutting to size, just leave them all a bit long and trim later, if you need to.

The frame has to be strong enough to assist the transition from woven sculpture to tree sculpture, so consider how you will join the wood. Posh joinery is not necessarily required, as the joins will probably not be seen: functionality is key.

◀ *"Living Willow Aurochs"* (c. 2004). *Benefitting from a sturdy frame of cleft oak, essential to secure the weighty oaken horns, the entire sculpture was constructed using materials gathered from the immediate area. Horns made by R. Stickland, using only hand tools.*

"Living Willow Aurochs" (c. 2006).   *Early summer. The presence of the aurochs in the carr is new but feels eternal, as if it had always been there. Born from the land, and of the land.*

"Living Willow Aurochs" (c. 2014). Before and after! The sculpture was left to revert to wild trees. The oak frame stands, the horns have fallen. All original weaving had disintegrated, and so was removed. All of the legs were growing, which provided plentiful withies to recreate the shape, restarting the sculpture with the benefit of established living willow.

"Living Willow Aurochs" (c. 2015). Ready for the second winter weave since the rebuild, the sculpture has recovered its shape, with living rods distributed evenly over the body. The lower living willow will be woven upward to strengthen the shell. Top growth will be pruned below the skin of the sculpture.

"Living Willow Aurochs" (c. 2016). Heading into summer, the aurochs resembles a green woolly mammoth, wandering through untamed wilderness.

Building the living willow sculpture

Internal frame

If you are making an independent internal frame, now is the time to build it and sink it into the ground. Before inserting living rods, create a shell around the frame, consistent with the shape of your sculpture. The latticed willow shell will hold the living leg sticks in place, the same way as it does in the goose, the pig, and the stag in this book.

External frame

The base shape will likely be more complex with an exoskeleton, in which case delineate the ground shape of where you are planning to plant the willow. I generally use a long piece of rope to represent the outer edge of the sculpture as it comes into contact with the ground. Your living willow will be set along this line, so consider the sunlight and space available to each plant-to-be in order to maximise its chances of survival. Most cuttings will survive if placed strategically, and the losses of a few should not matter in the long term. Think about staggering the planting for thickness of aerial growth while allowing distance between the plantings for root growth. You are aiming for even coverage of living willow over the whole of the sculpture, so it's important to consider density at the base of the sculpture to allow room for upward growth.

Branches that succeed may intertwine and graft together, creating, as years progress, densely twisted shapes. This process can be encouraged by making slits in the bark where living withies cross and binding them together (with willow ties) to prevent movement.

"Perching Eagles" (c. 2003). A hollow trunk was found, cut across, and used as two plinths for a pair of eagles. Living willow was planted through the trunk to allow direct growth up the legs, into the chest. The tail and wings of the bird reached the ground and were formed with living willow. No independent internal frame was necessary. An ash rod, reaching from the ground, through the hole in the perch, up to the oaken beak, held all in place while the willow grew around it.

◂ "Perching Eagles" (c. 2008). Summertime maintenance involved gently guiding the new growth through the existing weaving, to create a living shell.

▸ "Perching Eagles" (c. 2015). The form can be clearly seen during winter. Maintaining this sculpture is working well. The shape has become denser, and the form is well defined.

"Perching Eagles" (c. 2016). Green, feathery leaves appear in spring. Growth on an established plant is vigorous. Selective hand trimming, carefully, with secateurs, can take place throughout the summer.

Insert the living willow

When the frame is in place, think about the contact points of the living willow with the ground. This is simple with a quadruped, as the obvious points of planting will be at each foot, maybe the tail, and the head, if the animal is grazing. If you haven't done so already, grade your willow for ease of use. Put the thickest rods aside for the structure, medium for reinforcement, and fine weavers for ties, wraps, and detail. You may have a more extensive grading system than three piles, depending on the size of your project. If you find any oddities, put them to one side and consider how you can incorporate them into your sculpture for interest or effect.

Using your spike and lump hammer, pre-make the holes to a depth of at least 25 cm (10 inches). Insert the willow as you make the holes. You will have many unruly uprights sticking up. Consider the "belly" and the "back" of your willow rods, and angle your pilot holes in order to fully exploit the willow's natural preference for bending. The angle at which the rods are inserted into the ground will affect the final shape of the frame. You will likely need a combination of straight and curved lines in order to create the desired shape. Just as you have in the previous projects, utilise the natural bend to create effect. Concentrate on the main body. Don't worry about appendages to start with, as the priority at this stage is to create a strong shape that will act as the growing core of the plant sculpture.

When your rods are inserted and standing proud, they should be made a bit more sensible by performing a few rounds of pairing (see Chapter 4). Ensure that your weavers are never thicker than your uprights. The main rods are for shape, and the weavers are for reinforcement.

Bend the opposing living uprights gently into hoops, or whatever shape is relevant, twisting the end of each withy around the body of its opposing rod to bind them together at the correct size and shape. Use the finest willow for ties if necessary, to support the hoops.

Avoid kinking the willow, as the branch will not grow past the point of a kink. The willow will generally be living until it begins to bend in a downward direction. Bear in mind that the sculpture is going to get bigger, so, even with an external skeleton system, allow room for the build and for growth. Reinforce the wobbly hoop shape with rounds of pairing at intervals of about 30 cm (12 inches) between layers. The pairing will really help to fix the shape.

"Corfe Castle Dragon" (c. 2022). This sculpture was made in the same way as a living willow sculpture, with freshly cut willow inserted into the ground to create the shape before reinforcing with weavers. The dragon is basically a living willow tunnel.

"Corfe Castle Dragon" (c. 2022). The fiery colours of this dragon stand bright in the misty morning. The shape was reinforced, with enough space for new shoots to grow from the main structure. This sculpture was made using only freshly cut willow and a set of secateurs.

If any of the living rods break but you feel reluctant to replace them, you can trim them below the external line of the sculpture, to create a growing crown in a strategic place.

When your central core is stable, you can think about introducing the living willow rods that will be feeding the appendages of the sculpture. Slype the butt end of a structural-sized rod and weave into the body in a downward direction, so the thick end of the *Salix* can be inserted into the ground to root, while the tip end is sticking out in the direction of the appendage. Keep these rods as straight as possible, to encourage vigorous growth – up to 45° from the vertical is acceptable.

"Corfe Castle Dragon" (c. 2022). This dragon was not to be a living sculpture, so it was levered from the ground, gently working around the base. The weaving held the shape together, and the dragon was tipped onto its side, the excess rods trimmed, and a "foot border" inserted for strength and a firm bottom.

Creating the form

When the basic shape is secure, you can begin to add the curves, shapes, and lines that are indicative of what it is you are making. As you are creating a three-dimensional sculpture, it is crucial that you regularly check shapes and proportions from all vantage points. If you concentrate on one area of the sculpture without considering the whole, you will end up with a disproportionate and unbalanced finish. Consistent with the general method, create shapes with thick rods and reinforce with thinner rods.

Once the shape is firm, you no longer need pairing but can simply weave in and out. Just like sewing, use the butt end as the needle until the rod is secure, then weave the more flexible tip end into the shape. Alternate your weavers, so an equal number are behind and in front of your structural shaping sticks. The equal opposing pressure provided by alternate weaving strengthens the sculpture further. It is helpful to take your weaving in many directions, gradually creating a latticework over the sculpture. During this stage you are aiming for an even coverage that will hold the growers in place. Wherever there's a big gap, dissect it with a weaver.

Keep checking your reference pictures, and focus on the curving lines of the animal. These lines will heavily influence the finished qualities of the sculpture. Aim for an easy flow through the body, representing movement and muscle tone. Be sure not to over-fill any particular area with weavers, as you will need room for the living willow to find its way through gaps to sunshine.

Work around the sculpture, building it up evenly. If you begin to feel a bit lost, turn away, do something else for a bit, and have a look later with a fresh eye.

Add the head and appendages

When the body is strong, turn your attention to the head. I have found that building an independent skull, true to shape, and then adding it to the sculpture enables detailed positioning that can enhance the character of the creature. Look at pictures or skulls of the animal that you are creating for an idea of form and proportion, but do remember that weave will be added, so do not make it as large as its final size will be.

Begin making the skull by shaping a few "snowshoes" (see Chapter 4), tie them together, create a shape, and reinforce. Introduce the head shape to the neck area, threading some existing neck withies into it to hold it roughly in place until you are happy with the position. Fix with further weaving, and incorporate living willow – which you may be able to position to create green hair.

By this point you should have a strong form and a clear shape, with evenly distributed living willow rods held in place by weavers, which hopefully represents whatever it is you are aiming to make: amazing that somehow, out of the chaos that is a hundred whippy sticks, a unique creation is formed.

Finish the coverage

Progressively utilising finer withies, and using either single rods for a random weave effect or multiple rods for a more structured finish, continue working around the sculpture until you are happy that you have finished it, while ensuring enough gaps are left through which the living willow sprouts can grow.

Revel in satisfaction as you have created a nature-based sculpture that you have completed, but which now is free to continue its unique evolution as an intrinsic part of the local landscape.

Maintaining a living willow sculpture

As a living entity, your sculpture will grow in a manner shaped by environmental variables, one of those being the person who cares for it. Willow sculpture requires an empathic approach and absorbs the personality of the person who guides it. If you treat your willow sculpture like topiary, constantly clipping to create clearly defined shapes, the likelihood is that the willow will die. Hedge trimmers are the kiss of death for living willow sculptures. Willow is wild and free-flowing. She may allow you to work with her, but trying to contain her will only fail. Living willow sculptures are fluid beings, ever changing and rarely clearly defined. Living willow sculpture is not a medium of order, but more one of nurturing and creative chaos.

For the first few years, while the plants' root systems are developing, weed suppressant and water supply are necessary throughout the summer (see "Growing Willow" in Chapter 3). Growth will not be vigorous until the plants are established. New shoots can be very gently teased into the shape of the sculpture, trained in certain directions, and held in place by original wicker work. However, the shoots will be extremely fragile, so you may decide to let them grow for the summer and use those long lengths to weave during the winter, when the sap is down. This will allow you to take established, flexible withies into areas of the sculpture that need reinforcement. A combination approach would be ideal: weaving in the high shoots and leaving the lower ones to grow until the winter. Areas exposed to sunlight will grow more than shaded areas. Try to feed living willow into the shady areas of the sculpture to encourage uniform strength.

When maintaining living willow sculptures, it is essential to remember that willow always favours growing in an upward direction and rarely appreciates being kept down. A 45° angle from the upward vertical is fine, but by the time you get to horizontal, the plant will be less impressed and may choose to put its precious energy somewhere it can salute the sun.

As willow grows upwards, in order to achieve a dense body, growth must come from low down the sculpture. As with a flailed hedge, if trimming always takes place at the top and edges of the plant, the centre and bottom become gappy and weak.

To counter this predisposition, pruning some living willow low to the ground encourages new shoots that can be woven up, into the body. When the sculpture itself is pruned for shape, the cuts should be made below the surface of the skin, allowing the crowns to remain invisible while providing new growth to incorporate into the existing shape.

When the plant has become established, it will display enormous growth, and this is when you can begin to trim it, strategically, during the summer. I do not suggest you trim every withy but, rather, consider which ones should be left to enhance the shape the following winter. The plant will not appreciate you taking off too much growth, as it uses its leaves to gather the energy required to sustain its root, but willow will let you take some. When the plant is established, it will be advantageous to selectively remove growth during the summer, in order to enjoy the form and protect the structure from strong wind damage. By the time your living willow sculpture is mature, it will have herbage growing into it, be providing habitat for insects, have birds nesting in the sculpture's cavity, and likely have small mammals around its base.

Try to keep pictures of your sculpture through the seasons and, when you carry out maintenance, before-and-after pictures. Take some from the same position each time, so you have a photographic record of your ever-changing tree sculpture.

10

Weaving willow figures

Out of all the animals that grace this beautiful planet, people must surely be the most complicated. Capable of such love, compassion, and creativity, but also such cruelty, destruction, and hate. However, each one of us has a choice when it comes to our actions, and an influence on what reality we manifest.

So I close this book with willow people, and how we might choose to weave our way in the world. Willow, as an artistic medium, comes with its own symbolisms, which express ideas associated with the sculptural form, emotionally, energetically, and structurally.

The willow sculpture techniques used to make figures are no different from those already described in this book, so here I present a gallery, with discussions including explanations of the builds.

You will find your own way to represent how people stand on this Earth.

"The Lady of the Lake" (c. 2004). To begin the sculpture, a basic figure was made with willow, binding sticks together to resemble a scarecrow. Willow was added to represent skin on the hands and face, using a random weave technique. The dress was constructed using "stake and strand" basketry techniques, to represent the "warp and weft" of textile weaving.

"The Lady of the Lake" (c. 2004). This sculpture was commissioned with the remit of a Pre-Raphaelite feel; particular attention was paid to the flowing form of the fabric.

The Lady seemed lonely on the pool, so I added "Swan in Nest" (c. 2003), placed on an inflated inner tube. The boat was loosely moored, and the dress acted as a sail. The boat gently moved around the sheltered pool, as did the swan. Every moment had an unrepeatable quality, sometimes tranquil and clear, sometimes cloudy and turbulent. The Lady stood constant, amidst all the change, her companion well known for serenely gliding above water while paddling frantically below.

Photo by David and Carol Murkson

"Lady with Basket" (c. 2004). *Built upwards, like a basket, using "stake and strand" techniques to represent the "warp and weft", stripped white Somerset willow and ornamental red dogwood were used to weave the dress, the drape of the material made with woven folds. Head and shoulders were built and snuggly dropped into the bodice. Buff willow, a three-strand technique, accentuated the tanned, taught muscular structure of this strong woman. Her hair was made from Somerset steamed willow, which had been soaked and left to dry wrapped around rods to set the curl, before they were added to the sculpture. The basket was made of hedgerow materials, as, of course, this lady's basket would be. This is the lady who gathers, provides, and stands as part of the natural world.*

◄ "Lady with Basket" (c. 2004).

➤ "Lady with Basket" (c. 2004).

"Giant" (c. 2005). I struggle with this sculpture, I find it oppressive and overbearing . . . which I suppose was the intent. A "stick man" frame was built with coppiced ash poles, left long at the feet to allow fixture to ground or plinth. The muscular structure was gradually built around the frame and finished with the three-strand technique to accentuate the muscle. Based upon the Cerne Abbas Giant, in Dorset, but formed as a dark shadow, this sculpture represents the pervading patriarchy that overshadows rural England. Creativity is obviously possible, but the dominant force is destruction. I ended up burning this wicker man on a solstice fire.

"Nymph" (c. 2006). Sometimes it is really fun to sit next to a pile of freshly cut willow and just knock something up – just letting it flow! This was one of those "half-an-hour" exercises, begun with a couple of internal "snowshoes", the round ends becoming shoulders and the tied pointed ends leading down into the pelvis. Appendages were quickly added to the torso. I love the lithe and playful energy of the willow water spirit.

"Lady with Lurcher" (c. 2009). The huntress, the role of woman as provider, working with nature. The huntress takes what is required, as part of the global ecosystem, but no more. This sculpture was built as a basket, from the ground up, using "stake and strand" basketry techniques to represent the "warp and weft" of the textile dress, and the three-strand technique for the skin. She did have a barn owl accompanying her at one stage, bringing appropriate associated symbolism.

➤ **"Melangell and the Hares" (c. 2015).** Based on the legend of St. Melangell and personal experience, this sculpture explores woman's role in environmental protection. The legend of Melangell comes from the Welsh Marches, c. 7th century. A local prince and his mounted entourage were hunting hares with hounds. The dogs flushed out a hiding hare, who fled, pursued, to a hermitage inhabited by the lady, Melangell. When the prince caught up, he found the hare sheltering under the skirts of the lady, and the hounds refusing to go near her. I had a similar experience on the Dorset Downs when walking an ancient green lane with my horse and wagon. Some dogs flushed out a hare, and a frantic race ensued . . . the hare was coursed around the meadow, then turned towards me, running full pelt, and leapt into my arms, nestling as the hare in Melangell's arms. The dogs surrounded us, but did not come near. A surreal privilege, indeed, to be holding the hare. After some time I walked away from the dogs and gently released the hare, who calmly made its way back across the meadow. This sculpture began life as a naked female figure, built using the three-strand technique of white willow on a simple frame of coppiced ash poles. At first she was the light balance to the dark "Giant". Over time she became independent from the "Giant", and woven clothing was added, as protection for her, and so were the hares. Melangell and the hares are all finished in a three-strand technique, of buff willow, representative of the sinewy flesh, and further enhancing their connectivity. The dress is woven akin to textiles, the hair is plaits of withies. There could not be a more perfect medium for this sculpture than willow. Her eyes are all-seeing oak, the tree of knowledge and wisdom.

Conclusion

In this book we have discussed willow's place in the natural and managed landscape as a genus that provides exceptional nurturing attributes, benefitting many species. Absorb yourself in a withy bed, and you will meet many creatures. I hope that you will feel confident in growing and sourcing willow in a way that supports the regeneration of natural habitat and supports biodiversity.

I have shared with you ideas and techniques, developed and refined over decades, but there are other ways. In willow sculpture, nothing is "wrong" or "right" – as long as it works, it's good! If you can make a goose and a pig, you can make pretty much anything. Play with willow, be brave, try things out. Let your imagination flow, consistent with the creative, intuitive moon and water, with which willow is associated.

I have started you off with projects that are manageable for beginners, and I hope you have found the step-by-step guides clear and useful. You have been provided with the necessary information required to embark upon your own creations, large or small, growing or not. I have revelled in sharing my knowledge of the magnificence of established living willow sculptures and how they, we, and the wider environment benefit from years of positive interactions with humans.

We have explored willow as a healer, emotionally, spiritually, and pharmacologically. Willow is a plant that can help bridge a gulf between people and planet.

My wish throughout the book has been to emphasise the symbiotic relationship of people working with nature – to emphasise the positives. Enough of the colonialist attitude to our shared Earth!

By creating form with willow, we are celebrating the all-embracing, symbiotic connection of life on Earth. I hope that this book has deepened your relationship with willow, and that your journey with her will be as wondrous as mine.

Glossary

Annular ring shank nails: Nails with rings along the shank, which allow better grip.

Back: The side of a withy that offers resistance when bent.

Belly: The side of the withy that curves when bent.

Billhook: A tool with a sickle-shaped blade, with a sharp inner edge.

Bodkin: A pointed tool used for enlarging gaps in basketry; archaic weapon, like a dagger.

Bog: Freshwater wetland, with spongy ground and decaying plant matter.

Bolt: Traditional measurement of a bundle of willow.

Brown willow ("browns"): Cut willow that has dried.

Buff willow: Cut willow that has been boiled in its bark, then stripped, resulting in a light-brown-coloured withy.

Butt: Thick end of a withy.

Carr: Area of wetland that has been colonised by pioneer trees, especially willow, alder, and birch.

Coppice: *Noun:* area of woodland that is managed by periodic cutting. *Verb:* to cut the plant to ground level in order to stimulate growth.

Crown: The high-up cut part of a pollarded tree from which shoots grow. (See also stool.)

Cuttings: Pieces of the stem used for propagation.

Foot border: Basketry technique that strengthens the base with the addition of a border.

Gaia: From Greek mythology, Gaia is personification of the Earth, mother of all life.

Gaia hypothesis: Theory formulated and developed by James Lovelock and Lynn Margulis, which explores the interconnectedness of all life on Earth.

Green willow ("greens"): Freshly cut willow – no matter the colour of the bark!

GRT: "General rule of thumb", which in this book refers to beginning the sculpture process with thick willow rods, and decreasing the willow size gradually as the sculpture progresses.

Hedge laying: Traditional hedge-management technique, which involves removing the side growth and laying the tall, vertical growth down horizontally, thus creating a stock-proof barrier that is rich in biodiversity and offers a valuable rural resource.

Heorot: Old English word meaning deer, hart, or stag.

Herb: Here used as a medical herbalist term, to include any plant or fungus part that can be used medicinally.

Imbolc: Cross-quarter fire festival in the Pagan (Earth-based religion) calendar, halfway between winter solstice and spring equinox.

Keystone taxa: Biological group that offers support to biodiversity over-proportionate to their presence.

Kind willow: Willow that is easy to use.

Mellowing: Allowing willow an initial drying time to increase the usability. With soaked willow this involves wrapping in a damp cloth to allow the bark to become less slippery, while the inner withy remains wet and pliable. I also use the term for resting freshly cut materials under a hedge for a couple of weeks before use, which allows initial shrinkage and loss of the willow's most energetic springiness.

Nodes: Points on the stem where a bud is located, which may develop into flowers, leaves, stems, or roots.

Osier: Basketry willow.

Over-soaking: Leaving soaking willow submerged for too long, causing deterioration in quality.

Pairing: Pinching weave performed with two weavers alternately jumping over each other.

Pollard: Like coppicing, but higher up the tree. Traditionally seen on common land to allow a crop of withies above grazing height. Also used to mark the edges of waterways that flood.

Random weave: Technique used for covering the shell of the sculpture by weaving one withy at a time in various directions.

Round wood: Timber that is left in complete lengths, rather than planked for use.

Sap: Fluid containing water and nutrients that is transported around the plant: the "blood" of a tree, circulating most actively in spring and summer.

Short rotation coppice (SRC): Crop of perennials, planted at high density and harvested more frequently than every decade and allowed to regrow for future harvest.

Slype: Diagonal cut through a withy.

Snedding: Stripping the side shoots from a central rod; usually carried out with a billhook.

Somerset Rose: Ancient willow tie for securing bolts of willow.

Stake and strand: Basketry method of using weavers ("strands") around thicker structural sticks ("stakes").

Steamed willow: Cut willow that has been steamed, resulting in a very dark brown, sometimes black, bark colour.

Stipule: An anatomical part of a leaf, which is typically an outgrowth at the base of a leaf stalk.

Stool: The low-down cut part of a coppiced tree from which shoots grow. (See also crown.)

Taxon: Term for a biological grouping.

Three-strand technique: Multi-withy finishing technique in willow sculpture.

Tincture: Medicine made by extracting plant constituents in alcohol.

Tips: Tops of withies.

Unkind willow: Willow that is hard on your hands, or won't strip easily.

Weave: To pass withies in front and behind other withies.

Weaver: Withy that is passing in front of and behind a thicker upright.

White willow ("whites"): In this case not *Salix alba*, but cut willow, usually *S. triandra*, which has been allowed to stand in water until the spring, and then stripped of its bark to reveal the natural white of the inner sapwood.

Withy (plural: withies): Flexible rods of willow, appropriate for basketry. From the Old English "wiððe", meaning a flexible stick, used for binding.

Withy bed: Plantation of coppiced willow trees, usually harvested on an annual rotation.

A HERBAL BIBLIOGRAPHY

Brinker, F. (2001). *Herbal Contraindications and Drug Interactions* (4th edition). Oregon: Eclectic Medical Publications.

Brooke, E. (2019). *Traditional Western Herbal Medicine.* London: Aeon Books.

Council of Pharmaceutical Society of Great Britain (1911). *The Pharmaceutical Codex.* **www.henriettes-herb.com/search/node/willow**

Culpeper, N. (1653). *The Complete Herbal & English Physician Enlarged (1995 Edition).* Hertfordshire: Wordsworth.

European Medicines Agency (2017). *Assessment Report on* Salix *[Various Species Including S. purpurea L., S. daphnoides Vill., S. fragilis L.], Cortex.* London: EMA. Available at: www.ema.europa.eu/en/documents/herbal-report/final-assessment-report-salix-various-species-including-s-purpurea-l-s-daphnoides-vill-s-fragilis-l_en.pdf

Fisher, C. (2018). *Materia Medica of Western Herbs.* London: Aeon Books.

Ganora, L. (2009). *Herbal Constituents.* Colorado: Herbal Chem Press.

Griggs, B. (1997). *Green Pharmacy* (2nd edition). Vermont: Healing Arts Press.

Hill, J. (1812). *The Family Herbal.* **www.henriettes-herb.com/search/node/willow**

Kindred, G. (1995). *The Sacred Tree.* Derbyshire: Glennie Kindred.

Lilly, W. (1659). *Christian Astrology* (2nd edition).

Mahdi, J. G., Mahdi, A. J., Mahdi, A. J., & Bowen, I. D. (2006). The historical analysis of aspirin discovery, its relation to the willow tree and antiproliferative and anticancer potential. *Cell Proliferation,* Vol. 39, No. 2, pp. 147–156. Available at: **www.ncbi.nlm.nih.gov/pmc/articles/PMC6496865/#b6**

Ody, P. (1993). *Complete Medicinal Herbal.* London: Dorling Kindersley.

Pengelly, A. (2004). *The Constituents of Medical Plants* (2nd edition). Oxfordshire: CAB1.

Taylor, S. (2021). *The Humoral Herbal.* London: Aeon Books.

Warren-Davies, D. (1993). *An Introduction to Decumbiture – Part 1.* www.skyscript.co.uk/decumbiture1.html#1

Wickes Felter, H. (1922). *The Eclectic Materia Medica.* **www.henriettes-herb.com/search/node/willow**

Index

Index
alder, 11, 233
almond willow, Black Maul (*Salix triandra*), 49, 50, 235
anaphrodisiac, willow leaves as, 24
anatomy of willow, 53–54
anchoring, 61, 135
annular ring shank(s), 71
　nail(s), 71, 142, 233
antlers, 143, 154–155, 166, 178
　real, 153
aphids, honeydew, 34
appendage(s), of statues, 202, 210, 212, 214
ash, 11, 225, 228
　coppiced, 190
ash rod, 207
aspirin, 20
astrology, 17

back of withy, 40, 53, 233
badger(s), 36
"Badgers in the Meadow", 37
baler/baling twine, 152, 196
"Ballerina", 159, 161, 162
bark, willow:
　medicinal uses of, 22
　salicin content of, 24
barn owl(s), 19, 36, 227
"Barn Owl Quartering", 37
basketry, 49, 56, 61, 73, 201, 220, 227, 233–235
　stake and strand of, 62
basketry techniques, 66–68
bats, pipistrelle, 36
bees, 40
belly of withy, 40, 53, 233

bender life, 3
bender tent, 1
billhook, 142, 146, 201, 233, 235
binding wrap(s), 56, 136
biocides, 33, 34, 38
　chemical, 200
biodegradable mulches, 185
biofuel, 188
　willow as, 15
birch, 11, 233
Black Maul, almond willow (*Salix triandra*), 49, 50
black sooty mould, 34
blood thinners, pharmaceutical, 21–22
bodkin, 89, 233
bog/wetland, 233
bolt(s), 43, 48, 57, 200, 233, 235
brambles, 185
brown willow ("browns"), 49, 50, 233
buff willow, 44, 49, 50, 172, 223, 228, 233
butt(s) of withy, 54, 233
buzzard(s), 36

cable tie(s), 196, 197
canker, 33
canker sores, 33
carr(s), 11, 15, 203, 233
cattle, 45
　"Holstein", 163–165, 167
　"Living Willow Aurochs", 203–205
　"Roger's Bull", 173–175
chemical biocides, 33, 200
chemical warfare, 34
choleric (yellow bile) humour, 18
climatic conditions, 198

cloth, warp and weft of, 62
cockerel(s), 75
common, biodiversity of, 7
coppice/coppicing, 11, 35, 140, 233
   short rotation (SRC), 15, 32, 234
coppiced willow, 32, 33, 140, 177, 235
"Corfe Castle Dragon", 211–213
corkscrew willow (*Salix tortuosa*), 199
couch grass, 185
coverage, of living willow sculpture, 215
crayfish, white-clawed, 50
cross tie(s), 55–57, 110, 112
crown, willow:
   grown within sculpture, 212
   pollarded, 233
      rods growing from, 20, 29, 42
cutting(s), 233
   from gardens, 48
   from hedgerows, 45
   for living willow sculpture, 185, 200
   newly planted, 32
   planting, 31, 185
   used for planting withy bed, 7, 31, 33

Danish oil, 73
deer, 35, 36, 59, 145, 151, 156
   heorot, 36, 234
   "Roe Deer", 35
   "Stag", 157, 168, 169
   "White Willow Stag", 139
   willow, 139–155, 168, 177, 206, 234
Department for Environment and Rural
      Affairs (DEFRA), 46
design, transferring to materials, 202–205
detail, stag, adding, 153–156
docks, 185
"Doe", 157
dormice, 48
Dorset Downs, 228
dragon, "Corfe Castle Dragon", 211–213
drainage, living willow sculpture,
      requirements of, 184
drawing side profile of sculpture, 143–146
duck(s), 85, 98

eagles, 207
   "Perching Eagles", 208, 209

eared willow (*Salix aurita*), 23
ears:
   of animals, 127, 155
      weaving, 65–66
   pig, 132–134
   stag, 155
elephant(s), "Living Elephants", 170, 171
elm, 153
enclosure acts, 46
endoskeleton(s), 187, 201
environmental protection, woman's role in,
      228
exoskeleton(s), 187, 201, 206
external form of living willow sculpture,
      creating, 214

fertiliser(s), 32, 33
finishing:
   goose, 100–105
   pig, 127–137
flailed hedge, 139, 216
flail hedge cutters, mechanical, 139
flint, knapping, 201
flowers/aments, willow, medicinal uses of, 22
foot border, 213, 233
foot plates, 159, 166, 168
fossil fuels, 15
foundations:
   goose, 77–93
   pig, 108–114
foxes, 36
frame(s):
   external, of living willow sculpture, 206–209
   hedgerow, 139, 141, 168
   internal, 139–155, 163, 182, 187, 202
   of living willow sculpture, 206
   metal, 159–179
   table, 143, 146
frog(s), 38
fungal infection, 33, 34

Gaia, 141
Gaia hypothesis, 233
gardens, withies from, 48
general rule of thumb (GRT), 59, 63, 76, 89,
      107, 112, 113, 127, 147, 149, 166, 200,
      234

"Giant", 225, 228
glyphosate, 34
"Golden Unicorn", 182, 183
golden willow, 177
goose/geese, 4, 71, 206
goose, willow, 139, 231
    creating shape, 79–89
    finishing, 100–105
    foundations, 77–93
    reinforcing shape, 88–93
    weaving, 75–106
green willow ("greens"), 40, 49, 50, 73, 233
"Growling Wolf", 195
GRT: *see* general rule of thumb

hare(s), 19, 26, 36
    "Leaping Hare", 179
    "Living Willow Hare", 188, 189
    "Melangell and the Hares", 228
    "Moongazing Hare", 21
harvesting, 29, 39, 40, 142
hazel, 140, 141, 151, 153
    cleft, 146
    coppiced, 139
hazel rods, 140
hedge(s):
    flailed/flailing, 46, 139, 216
        annual, 47
    as habitat, 46
    laid, 234
        traditionally, 47, 139
    withies from, 45–48
hedge laying, 234
hedgerow, 139, 140, 141, 168, 223
    frame, 139, 141, 168
hens, 75
heorot (deer, stag), 36, 234
herbalism, 7
herbal medicine, 17, 18, 20, 22, 26
herbs (medicinal), 24, 234
herons, 75
Higgins, Lindsay, 157
"Holstein", 163–165, 167
honeydew, aphid, 34
horse(s), 59, 228
    "Shire Horse and Seeker", 197–199
"Howling Wolves", 181, 190–195

humoral medicine, 17, 18
humour:
    choleric (yellow bile), 18
    melancholic (black bile), 18
    phlegmatic (phlegm), 18, 22, 26
    sanguine (blood), 18

Imbolc, 26, 34, 234
internal frame, role of, 139–155, 163, 182, 187, 202, 206

join(s), laid-in, 67
joint(s):
    nailed, 71
    screwed, 71

keystone taxon/taxa, 14, 234

"Lady of the Lake", 220, 221
"Lady with Basket", 223, 224
"Lady with Lurcher", 227
laid-in join(s), 67
leaf nodes, 31
    rootlets from, 185
"Leaping Hare", 179
leaves, willow, medicinal uses of, 22, 24
legs, creating:
    goose, 94–99
    pig, 115–126
    stag, 151
leverets, 36
life–death–rot–rebirth cycle, 190
little owls, 36
"Living Elephants", 170, 171
living shell, creating, 208
"Living Willow Aurochs", 203–205
"Living Willow Hare", 188, 189
living willow sculpture(s), 166, 181–217, 231
    affected by:
        microclimate, 186
        obstacles, 186–187
    awkward teenage years of, 187, 194
    building, 206–215
    coverage of, 215
    creating external form of, 214
    external frame, 206–209
    head and appendages of, 214–215

living willow sculpture(s) (*continued*):
   internal frame of, 206
   locating, 184–200
   maintaining, 215
   outcompeted by weeds, 185–186
   planning, 201–205
   requirements of, 184
      drainage, 184
      rooting, 185
      soil, 184
   summer pruning, 189
   transferring design to materials, 202–205
   weaving living willow into frame, 210–213
living willow tunnel, 211
Lovelock, James, 233
lunar cycle and menstrual cycle, relationship between, 19
lurcher(s), 59
   "Lady with Lurcher", 227

Margulis, Lynn, 233
melancholic (black bile) humour, 18
"Melangell and the Hares", 228
mellow(ing), 50, 51, 234
menstrual cycle, 19, 24
   and lunar cycle, relationship between, 19
metal frame(s), 159–179
   making, 163–171
   planning, 160–162
   preserving, 172–179
   template for shaping, 162
   with wire reinforcement, 173
microclimate, living willow sculpture affected by, 186
micro-plastics, 186
molecular fingerprint, willow's, 20
monoculture, 15
moon, 14, 19–26, 140, 231
   representing the feminine, 19
   willow's relationship with, 19
"Moongazing Hare", 21
mortise-and-tenon joints, 141, 142
   round wood, 69
mould, black sooty, 33
mulches, biodegradable, 185
muscular structure, 166, 223, 225
musculoskeletal system, stag's, 147

nail(s), 71, 146
   annular ring shank, 142, 233
nailed joint(s), 71
nerve agent, 34
nettles, 185
node(s), 200, 234
   leaf, 31, 185
non-growing willow sculptures, 166
"Nymph", 226

oak, 11, 228
   cleft, 203
oak frame, 204
obstacles, living willow sculpture affected by, 186–187
oil treatment, UV-protection, 172
orange rust, 33
organophosphate, 34
ornamental willows, 48
osier(s), 29, 40, 49, 148, 200, 234
   importing of, 15
   size grading, 43
over-soaking, 50, 234
owl(s):
   "Barn Owl Quartering", 37
   little, 36
   "Owl on Oak", 19
   tawny, 36
   "Winter Owl Hunting", 20
"Owl on Oak", 19

pain relief through salicylates, 24
pair(ing), 66, 210, 214, 234
pathogens, 33–34
   plant, 200
peacocks, 75
"Perching Eagles", 207, 208, 209
phlegmatic (phlegm) humour, 18, 22, 26
phytochemicals, 22
pictures, reference, 142, 147, 151, 160, 201, 214
pig, willow, 139, 206, 231
   ears, 132–134
   finishing, 127–137
   foundations, 108–114
   legs, 115–126
   reinforcing shape, 112
   snout, 130–131

tail, 135–136
    weaving, 107–137
"Pig", 107, 137
pinching weave, 61, 66
pioneer trees, 233
    willow as, 11
pipistrelle bats, 36
plant pathogens, 200
plinth(s), 71–72, 75, 98, 145, 225
pollard/pollarding, 29, 233, 234
preserving:
    metal frame(s), 172–179
    non-growing willow, 72
    willow sculpture, 72
pruning, summer, 189, 216
purple willow (*Salix purpurea*), 22
pussy willow, 40

rabbits, 35, 36
random weave, 62–63, 137, 156, 215, 220, 234
red oxide, 168
reference pictures, 142, 147, 151, 160, 201, 214
"Reindeer", 178
reinforcing shape:
    goose, 88–93
    pig, 112
    stag, 149
rheumatism, 26
ring shank(s), annular, 71
    nails, 71, 142, 233
River Wey, 1
"Rob", 176, 177
"Roe Deer", 35
"Roger's Bull", 173–175
rooting, living willow sculpture, requirements of, 185
round wood, 71, 141, 146, 234
round wood mortise and tenon, 69
rust, 34
    orange, 33
    preventing, 166, 168

salicylate(s), 20–22, 24
salicylate-containing plants, 26
salicylic acid, 20
Salix (genus), 14, 22
Salix alba (white willow), 22, 235

Salix aurita (eared willow), 23
Salix babylonica (weeping willow), 199
Salix purpurea (purple willow), 22
Salix tortuosa (corkscrew willow), 199
Salix triandra (Black Maul), 49, 50, 235
sanguine (blood) humour, 18
sap, 140, 200, 216, 234
    medicinal uses of, 22
screw(s), 71, 142, 146, 197
screwdriver, 89
screwed joint(s), 71
sculpture(s):
    techniques, willow, 59–66
    two sides of, as mirror images, 146
    see also: living willow sculpture(s); willow sculpture(s); willow sculpture techniques
sculpture strangulation, 196
secateurs, 142, 201, 209
self-holding tie(s), 55, 120
shape, creating:
    goose, 79–89
    stag, 147–152
"Sheep on Holway Hill", 141
"Shire Horse and Seeker", 197–199
short rotation coppice (SRC), 15, 32, 234
shrimps, fresh-water, 50
size grading, 44
    osiers, 43
skeleton, 187, 202, 210
slype, 65, 68, 128, 130, 132, 135, 212, 235
snedding, 142, 201, 235
snout, pig, 130–131
snowshoe(s), 59–60, 109–112, 115, 123, 124, 130, 215, 226
soaking tank, 45
soaking times, for withies, 44
soil conditions, 198
soil erosion, 186
soil moisture, 32
soil requirements of living willow sculpture, 184
soil type(s), 184, 196, 202
Somerset Levels, 49, 50, 57
Somerset Rose, 43, 57–59, 235
sooty mould, black, 33, 34
spring equinox, 26, 234

SRC: *see* short rotation coppice
stag, 168, 177, 206, 234
    detail, adding, 153–156
    drawing side profile of, 143–146
    finishing, 156
    frame, constructing, 143–146
    legs, creating, 151
    musculoskeletal system of, 147
    shape:
        creating, 147–152
        reinforcing, 149
    weaving, 139–155
"Stag", 157, 168, 169
stake and strand basketry, 62, 220, 223, 227, 235
steamed willow, 49, 50, 141, 223, 235
stipule, 235
St. Melangell, 228
stool, 29, 35, 40, 54, 233, 235
    willow, coppiced, life expectancy of, 33
summer pruning, 189
swan(s), 75, 85, 222
    "Swan in Nest", 222
symmetrical weaving, on both sides of sculpture, 93

table frame, 143, 146
tail, pig, 135–136
tannins, 22, 24, 26, 49
tawny owls, 36
taxon/taxa, 14, 235
tension strap, 77, 80
    top, 81
tension weaver, 81, 82
three-strand technique, 62, 63, 103, 104, 137, 174, 223, 225, 227, 228, 235
tie(s):
    cross, 55–57, 110, 112
    self-holding, 55, 120
    willow, 54, 196, 206
tincture, 26, 235
tip(s), 43, 54, 63, 122, 133, 146, 151, 156, 235
    tying in, 57
toad(s), 36
trimming, hand, selective, using secateurs, 209
tuberculosis, 24

twig(s), willow, medicinal uses of, 22, 24
twisting withies, 54
tying in tip(s), 57

ultraviolet protection, 73
unicorn(s), 4, 182
    "Golden Unicorn", 182, 183
    "White Willow Unicorn", 51
UV protection, 172

vinegar, 26

warp and weft of cloth, 62
waterproofing, 73
wax treatment, 172
weave:
    pinching, 61, 66
    random, 62–63, 137, 156, 215, 220, 234
weaver(s), 154
    tension, 81, 82
    wrapping, 136
weaving, 55, 61, 62, 67, 71, 73
weaving techniques, 53–73
weeds, living willow sculpture outcompeted by, 185–186
weeping willow (*Salix babylonica*), 199
wetland/bog, 233
Wey Navigation Canal, 1
white willow (*Salix alba*), 22, 235
white willow ("whites"), 22, 44, 49, 50, 141, 142, 154, 174, 175, 228, 235
    stripped, 172
"White Willow Stag", 139
"White Willow Unicorn", 51
whittling, 68–69
willow(s):
    almond (*Salix triandra*), Black Maul, 49, 50, 235
    anatomy of, 53–54
    associated with water, 184
    bio-fuel, 188
    brown ("browns"), 49, 50, 233
    buff, 44, 50, 172, 223, 228, 233
    cooling character of, 19
    eared (*Salix aurita*), 23
    fresh, 75
    golden, 177
    green ("greens"), 40, 50, 73, 233

growing, 29–35
  investment in, 15
healing properties of, 17–26
healing qualities of, 231
kind, 44, 234
ornamental, 48
pre-dried and soaked, 75
purple (*Salix purpurea*), 22
steamed, 49, 50, 141, 223, 235
unkind, 235
weaving, therapeutic character of, 20
weeping (*Salix babylonica*), 199
white (*Salix alba*), 22, 235
white ("whites"), 49, 50, 141, 142, 154, 174, 175, 228, 235
white stripped, 44, 172
working with, therapeutic values of, 4
willow bark, 24–26
  as medicine, 21
  stripped, 25
willow figures, weaving, 219–229
willow merchants, withies from, 48–50
willow people, 219
willow sculpture(s):
  "Badgers in the Meadow", 37
  "Ballerina", 159, 161, 162
  "Barn Owl Quartering", 37
  "Corfe Castle Dragon", 211, 212, 213
  "Giant", 225, 228
  "Golden Unicorn", 182, 183
  "Growling Wolf", 195
  "Holstein", 163, 164, 165, 167
  "Howling Wolves", 190–195
  "Lady of the Lake", 220, 221
  "Lady with Basket", 223, 224
  "Lady with Lurcher", 227
  "Leaping Hare", 179
  "Living Elephants", 170, 171
  "Living Willow Aurochs", 203–205
  "Living Willow Hare", 188, 189
  "Melangell and the Hares", 228
  "Moongazing Hare", 21
  "Nymph", 226
  "Owl on Oak", 19
  "Perching Eagles", 207, 208, 209
  "Pig", 107, 137
  "Reindeer", 178
  "Rob", 176, 177
  "Roe Deer", 35
  "Roger's Bull", 173–175
  "Sheep on Holway Hill", 141
  "Shire Horse and Seeker", 197–199
  "Stag", 157, 168, 169
  "Swan in Nest", 222
  "White Willow Stag", 139
  "White Willow Unicorn", 51
  "Winter Owl Hunting", 20
willow sculpture techniques:
  basic, 59–66
  established, maintaining, 186
  figures, weaving, 219–229
  goose, 75–106
  living, 181–217
    locating, 184–200
  metal frames, 159–179
    making, 163–171
    planning, 160–162
    preserving, 172–179
  non-growing, 166
    preserving, 72
  pig, 107–137
  stag, 139–155
    antlers, 153
    detail, adding, 153–156
    ears, 155
    frame, making, 143–146
    legs, 151
    shape, creating, 147–152
willow stool, coppiced, life expectancy of, 33
willow ties, 196, 206
willow tunnel, living, 211
"Winter Owl Hunting", 20
winter solstice, 234
wire, 196, 197
wire twist, 196
Wisley Woods, 1
withy(ies):
  back of, 40, 233
  "back" or "belly", curves created by, 147
  belly of, 40, 53, 233
  cutting, 41
  harvesting, 29, 39, 40, 142
  plaited, 228
  preparation of, 50–51

withy(ies) (*continued*):
   size grading of, 44
   soaking times for, 44
   sorting and storing of, 43–45
   sourcing, 29–51
      from gardens, 48
      by growing, 29–35
      from hedges, 45–48
      from willow merchants, 48–50
withy bed(s), 7, 31, 33, 197, 231, 235
   harvesting, 39–41
   managing, 34–38
   planting in rows, 29
   removal of, 15
wolf/wolves, "Howling Wolves", 190–195
woman's role in environmental protection, 228
wood, round, 71, 141, 146, 234
woodpeckers, 36
woodwork, 68–72
wrap(s):
   binding, 56, 136
   willow, 54
wrapping weaver(s), 136